BROOK AND RIVER TROUTING

HARFIELD H. EDMONDS
NORMAN N. LEE

Coch-y-Bonddu Books
2009

BROOK AND RIVER TROUTING
EDMONDS & LEE

First published privately by the authors in 1916
Reprinted in facsimile - Orange Partridge Press 1980
Reprinted in facsimile - Smith Settle 1997

New edition published by The Flyfisher's Classic Library 2009
This paperbound edition published by Coch-y-Bonddu Books Ltd 2009

New Introduction © 2009 Oliver Edwards
© 2009 The Flyfisher's Classic Library
An imprint of
Coch-y-Bonddu Books Ltd, Machynlleth, Powys SY20 8DG
01654 702837
www.ffcl.com   www.anglebooks.com

ISBN 978-1-904784-19-7

INTRODUCTION TO 2009 EDITION

By the time I started work in 1953 I was already smitten by flyfishing, which is odd since my background was coarse fishing on the Northern Working Men's Club match fishing scene. Odder still, I had never been flyfishing, hadn't even held a fly rod, and had only a vague idea of how to go about it. My father - a coarse fisherman - was no help either; strongly hinting that I should continue float fishing. My uncle Harry a "crack" matchman and member of the Leeds "All England" team would, I was sure, know something about flyfishing. But he didn't. I was, it seemed, on my own.

But fate's hand was soon to rest on my shoulder. Within a few months of starting work I was informed that apparently there was someone in the Drawing Office who went flyfishing. That someone was Angus Owen Smith and no magnet had greater attraction. So yes, it soon happened, I was taken flyfishing.
The important thing to bear in mind is the period – the early fifties. For river fly fishermen then, the choice of fly appeared to be quite uncomplicated; at least it did to me. You fished three spiders - a team - if they failed, well…. you tried different spiders!

Fortunately it was possible in those days to buy beautifully tied North-Country Spiders, correct to the dressing recipe, and correct in the important "sparse style". In Leeds, where I was apprenticed, the gunsmith's, Linsley's, in Albion Street had the best selection, and every time the beautifully varnished multi-compartmented box was opened before me, I drooled. Their strange names - Dark Watchet, Poult Bloa, Dark Needle, Rough Bodied Poult, Light Snipe etc, - just added to the magic of it all. Angus enthused about spiders, and much of his conversation centred on them and "stickles" (riffles). Angus's enthusiasm for spiders quickly gripped me – you bet it did. This fifteen year old lad was now and again getting his rod bent by a trout or a grayling which had grabbed one of these tiny scraps of feather.

Angus had a note-book which interested me, and from time to time I'd get a peek inside it. It was within this note-book that I first saw the pencilled words *Brook & River Trouting*. As I recall, it actually said "*....Patterns from Brook & River Trouting.....*" followed by a list of Angus's favourites.

"Don't even think about it...." as I started to ask the obvious question, "......you can't get the book, only a few have it, it's unobtainable, and only a few were ever printed. I once saw a copy; it's fantastic, it's got colour pictures of the flies and it also shows all the materials used on each fly. It's even got a list of flies you should use each month; it's the spider Bible". And so he went on... and on and on... about this mythical book which was so rare you couldn't possibly buy one! So that was that, forget about it, you can't buy it, forget it......but I couldn't. Angus had whetted my appetite too well; *Brook and River Trouting* was gnawing away at me.

At that time I would often spend my lunch hour in Leeds City Library, questing for anything on flyfishing. One lunch hour I discovered that the library had a special reference department, and I was also told that they may have some old fishing books! So up I went to the top floor, and, almost tingling with hope dared to ask..... "I don't suppose you have a copy of *Brook and River Trouting* by Edmonds & Lee, do you?" .... "I'll just check"..... said the lady librarian. Remember I was nobbut a lad of fifteen and anything about flyfishing was grist to my mill, but this book, this "bible" I just had to see – would they have it? PLEASE have it.

I can still see the librarian approaching me now, clutching this smallish dull chestnut-brown book....could this really be it? I could hardly believe my luck; a copy was here all the time, languishing on some dusty shelf a mile from where I worked. So here was the book I would never ever see, opened before me. Angus had undersold it, it was far better than any picture my mind had painted. Unfortunately it was not for borrowing - this was the reference department, you only looked! So, this garret was where I spent many, many lunch hours – "devouring" *Brook and River Trouting.* That's how it happened, my personal discovery of this "lost" classic, and in the years that followed, my copied notes of all the dressings were extremely well used, with the patterns from Linsley's as my tying guide.

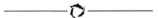

Edmonds & Lee pulled off three masterstrokes for the flytyer, the most important being the photographs of the materials required for each fly. These were grouped alongside the photograph of each and every fly, thus at a stroke, eliminating any guesswork for those all important hackles. For instance, you can actually overlay your greyish barred feather from the under coverts of a woodcock's wing, and be certain you've got the correct one for the Winter Brown. Then there is the often perplexing problem of where to find the required hackle feather on the actual bird, the various covert feathers. This is shown in clear detail using a pair of well labelled snipe wings, both upper and under sides. Where feathers from other parts are called for – thigh, flank, base of tail, etc - there can be little error, the photographs have this clearly covered. The final masterstroke, I believe, is their inclusion of a colour chart of the full range of Pearsall's "Gossamer" silks. This is particularly important today when newcomers to tying North Country flies are striving to find original "Gossamers" on wooden spools (now becoming a "sport" of its own) or are forced to find alternative brands of pure silk thread.

There is no doubt in my mind that *Brook and River Trouting* was a scarce book from the start for a few obvious reasons. First of all, it was expensive, thirty shillings is said to have been its price on publication. Thirty shillings was a lot of money for a flyfishing book in 1916, a week's wage for a working man in fact. Secondly, there were relatively few printed. So it is easy to imagine that a book with such information and appeal would only find its way onto the bookshelves of the more affluent. Remember also, this book was published when the "Great War" was at its bloodiest. In 1916 the battles of the Somme and Verdun were raging; the entire country was losing thousands of its men; there were even some small villages left almost bereft of their men folk! So ask yourself this. Who, back in "Blighty", would be fortunate enough to be indulging themselves in the gentle pursuit of flyfishing during this awful time? There is every chance that the book would have remained in the hands of a few privileged people who would have been very impressed by the precise and detailed information it contained. The book would have been treasured and kept and consequently, for many, many years, second-hand copies were a rare find – and expensive. But now things have changed; the Internet with its many second-hand and specialist book dealers has seen to that, and first editions, it seems, are becoming just a little less scarce than they were twenty years ago. Nevertheless they still command a high price; into the hundreds for a good "tight" copy. Twenty years ago even a reasonably good copy would have cost at least £250, (as I found out, I told my wife it was £50!) and a poor condition "loose" first edition would have been around £100.

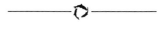

So the years rolled by. Then in late 1979, completely out of the blue, I was approached by the Orange Partridge Press to write the introduction to a new edition. Twenty-six years had passed since I first gazed at the book and carefully copied down all those dressings. *Brook and River Trouting* was going to be available again at long last, and fly fishers would once again have the dressings of these unique flies, the picture of each fly, and those all important pictures of the materials for tying each fly. This facsimile limited second edition was published in 1980. The thirst for this book remained unquenched and a third edition was published by Smith Settle in Otley in 1997.

Now, thirty years after the Orange Partridge Press edition, I find myself once again writing about a book which has played a significant part in my flyfishing life. Although I may be associated with tying what some refer to as "close copy" patterns, my great love is still tying and fishing these sparse classic North-Country flies, and, unless there is something really specific happening – hatch-wise - these timeless patterns are, as the Americans say, my GO TO patterns.

On streamy water, where aquatic insects emerge and terrestrial insects fall, the patterns within the pages of this book are as near guaranteed to deceive trout and grayling as anything in flyfishing can ever be guaranteed – wherever trout streams flow.

Oliver Edwards,
Carlton,
Wakefield,
February 2009.

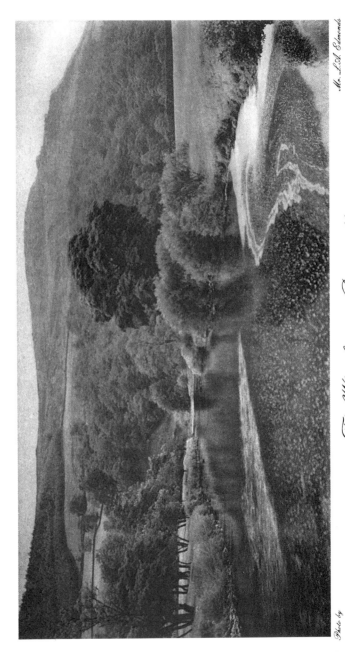

Photo by   Mr. L. S. Edmonds.

The Wharfe near Burnsall.

BROOK AND RIVER TROUTING

A Manual of modern North Country methods

With Coloured Illustrations of Flies
and Fly-Dressing Materials

By
HARFIELD H. EDMONDS
NORMAN N. LEE

PUBLISHED BY THE AUTHORS, 23, BANK STREET, BRADFORD.

CONTENTS.

		PAGE.
PREFACE		5
CHAPTER I.	Flies. Table I. Table II. Dressings ...	7
CHAPTER II.	Fly Fishing. Wet-Fly Fishing. Dry-Fly Fishing...	31
CHAPTER III.	Creeper and Stone Fly Fishing	62
CHAPTER IV.	Upstream Worm Fishing	69
CHAPTER V.	Minnow Fishing...	91
INDEX		103

ILLUSTRATIONS.

FRONTISPIECE: The Wharfe near Burnsall

Snipe's Wing, Inner side	8
Snipe's Wing, Outer side	8
Shades of Silk	10
Drawings of Natural Flies	12
Flies with Dressing Materials	16 et seq.
A Typical Stretch...	30
Headwaters of the Aire	46
Broken Water	60
The Head of the Dale	76
A Brook in Spring	96

PREFACE.

WHEN the writers began to take a practical interest in trout fly dressing, they experienced great difficulty in determining the correct feathers for the various patterns, as the older books on the subject of North Country flies are vague in the extreme. The few more modern writers on wet flies, for want of precision, have done little to help the beginner to a proper appreciation of his materials. It was therefore felt that a book, which not only prescribed the exact part of a bird from which the correct feathers should be taken, but illustrated such feathers and other materials (as also the flies made therefrom), in colour, would be a help, at least to beginners in the craft, and not merely an encumbrance on angling literature.

Having conceded the difficulties of the novice wishing to dress his own flies, the question of the number of patterns necessary for fishing the Rivers of the North Country naturally came next for consideration. As the tendency during recent years has been to increase the number out of all reason and beyond practical bounds, to the great bewilderment of the beginner and the occasional fisherman, a list of flies has been drawn up which, while it contains few patterns as compared with many other lists, is yet wide enough to provide for varying conditions the season through. The flies are for the most part old friends, but for the above reasons it is hoped they will not be unwelcome.

The original scheme of this work was limited by the foregoing considerations. But when the book had been mapped out in a general form it became evident that a description of the methods employed in fishing North Country streams with success would not only give point to what the writers had to say on flies, but might be of interest to the majority of North Country fishermen. It was therefore decided to enlarge the scope of the work. The chapters on the various methods of fishing the Rivers of the Northern Counties are the outcome of practical experience, and as such it is hoped they will be both useful and interesting.

The authors desire to express their indebtedness to Mrs. A. R. Gurney, Mr. L. A. Edmonds, and Mr. F. Creedy for the photographs from which several of the river scenes have been reproduced.

H. H. E.

1916.   N. N. L.

CHAPTER I.

FLIES.

WHILE it is the endeavour of this work to bring the range of trout flies within reasonable and practical limits and to describe no other than sound practical dressings, there is no desire to limit experiment either in patterns or numbers. In fact to do so would take away one of the pleasantest features of the pastime and rob many a winter's evening of its delight. All those who take an interest in fly dressing should work from Nature wherever possible, for flies frequently differ in no small degree in different localities ; and there is a great deal of enjoyment to be obtained in dressing a fly with the natural insect before one, and afterwards killing trout on the resulting work of one's hands.

It is not intended to devote any space to the processes of fly-tying, as much has been written on the subject. The reader in search of information cannot do better than read the late H. G. McClelland's book, *The Trout Fly Dresser's Cabinet of Devices, or How to tie Flies for Trout and Grayling Fishing,* which is the most practical and exhaustive treatise on the subject known to the writers.

The illustrations, facing this page, of both sides of a Snipe's wing will show the reader the precise places from which the various wing feathers, described in the text, are taken, and while the descriptions of the feathers may not satisfy the naturalist, they are sufficient for the purposes of the writers.

It is naturally of importance in fly-dressing to use no hooks but the best, and it will be found that Hardy Bros.' tapered snecks are satisfactory in every respect, except that they are on the long side. If about one-sixteenth of an inch be cut off the shank with an old pair of scissors before dressing the fly, a more useful length will be attained, as artificial flies are much more killing if kept short in the body. Stress is laid on this ; and it will be seen from the illustrations of the flies that the tail ends of the bodies are not carried further down the hook than half way between the point of the hook and the point of the barb. For the two floating Spinners, Hardy Bros.' Dry Fly Eyed Hooks are recommended. The numbers of the hooks given in the text correspond with the numbers enumerated in Hardy Bros.' catalogue.

The writers prefer to dress their flies to gut, 4x being the most suitable grade ; but good hair, if it can be obtained, will be found delightful to fish with, as a cast made

Inner side

Outer side

from it falls so very lightly on the water; and, even when the hair has become thoroughly soaked, the droppers, unlike those tied to gut, have no tendency to twist round the cast, but stand well out from it.

The most satisfactory tying silk is Pearsall's "Gossamer," which is standardized in shades. A shade card is illustrated and the numbers appearing after the various silks mentioned in the text correspond with the numbers above the various shades illustrated.

In dressing the flies the silk is in all cases waxed with transparent wax; and, where it is stated that such and such a silk is to be well waxed, the result should be a shade or two darker than an ordinary waxing would give.

In the dressings of most of the winged flies it is laid down that either the outer side or the inner side of the quill feather used should in the finished article appear as the "under side" of the wing of the artificial. The reader will easily understand which is the "under side" of the wing of the artificial if he remembers that it is that side of the wing which would touch the water if the fly were " spent " and floating thereon.

Although the primary quill feathers are almost exclusively recommended for the wings of most of the winged patterns, the secondaries will often do equally well.

The correct shade of dubbing for the bodies of flies, where coloured dubbing is specified, can often be obtained to most advantage by a mixture of two or more shades. For instance, the dubbing for the Winter Brown is a mixture of brown and maroon wool, while the dubbing for the Green Insect is a mixture of green and yellow wool.

The silks forming the heads of the various flies are of the same shade as the respective silks used for the bodies unless otherwise stated; and it should be borne in mind that the flies, particularly the hackle patterns, must be dressed lightly, if one of the most distinctive features of the North Country patterns is to be preserved. In copying from Nature let the imitation err on the small side if anything.

No attempt has been made to reproduce in the coloured plates either gold or silver wire or tinsel.

When the river is "coloured," flies dressed a size larger than those employed under normal conditions can be used with advantage.

Although the seasons for the various flies are given, they are approximate only, as districts frequently vary one from another, and the lateness or otherwise of a season naturally has an effect on the hatch, just as it has on the roses in gardens. Often the March Brown can be seen in the latter part of May, and sometimes a particular fly, for no apparent reason, will remain on the water for a longer time than usual. The necessity of careful observation cannot therefore be too strongly impressed, as observation will teach far more than all the books that were ever written.

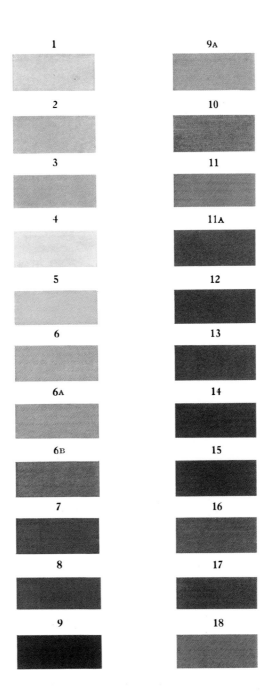

Shades of Silk.

The form of wing specified for the Spinners is recommended to the attention of the reader, as being a most practical form of wing for any winged pattern, wet or dry, where transparency is the primary object. To the writers it seems an improvement on the hackle points now so popular for many flies, as it is free from the objectionable and comparatively thick midrib of the latter and it is a harder wearing dressing than the older form. The development to which such newer form of wing lends itself for other patterns than the Spinners mentioned in the list at pages 24, 26 and 30 may be noted, and the field which is open for experiment will be evident to the reader.

Under the name of each fly, in giving its dressing, the name of the order or family to which the natural insect as represented by the artificial belongs will be found, and opposite page 12 reproductions of typical examples of each of the orders or families of natural insects mentioned will be found, with the exception of the Ant and Green Insect. The latter are so well known as to need no illustration. The beginner will therefore have an idea of the fly he is copying and perhaps be able to identify it at the stream side. It must not be forgotten however that certain patterns represent more than one species of fly.

It has been the good fortune of the writers to fish on many waters; and while the Winter Brown has often given them the first thrill of the season, and the Green Insect accounted for fish when September gusts have strewn the river with leaves and green fly, they hope they have not grown dogmatic in their views and opinions on matters piscatorial. Nevertheless they are inclined to think that, the closer they keep in shade and colour in their patterns to the natural flies, the greater has been their success ; for, although they can recall occasions on which the fish would rise at almost anything, such occasions have been few and far apart ; while the times when the trout would only look at a particular fly of a particular shade have been by far the more frequent in their experience. Why deny fish the power to appreciate variations of shade when they live in a world of colours, and are clothed in such a beautiful and vari-coloured mail ? If trout can appreciate tones of colour, how different a fly must appear to them in different lights and with different backgrounds. Such natural variations of surrounding light and landscape may have a larger effect on " the bag " than many think.

For easy reference two tables of flies are given. One, in which are set down the flies in the order in which they may generally be fished through the season, with the approximate times of their use, and the other, with the flies tabled under the various trout fishing months.

It remains only to add, that the taking fly should be fished as point, *i.e.*, the fly farthest from the angler.

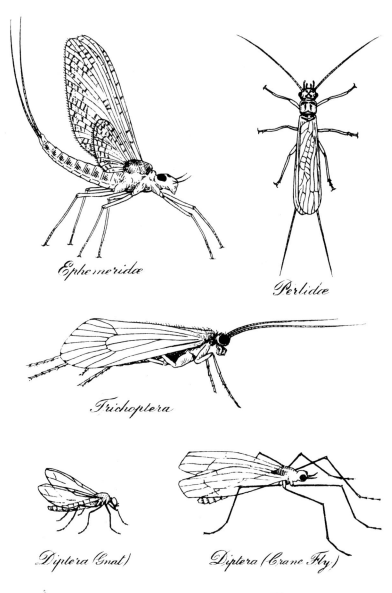

Ephemeridæ

Perlidæ

Trichoptera

Diptera (Gnat)

Diptera (Crane Fly)

Natural Flies of the Orders & Families named

TABLE I.

1. Winter Brown .... March to middle of April.
2. Waterhen Bloa ...... March to end of April and again in September.
3. Greenwell's Glory .... March to first week in May and again in September.
4. Spring Black .... March and early April.
5. Dark Snipe .... March to middle of April and again in September.
6. Orange Partridge .... March to middle of May.
7. Broughton's Point .... March to middle of April.
8. March Brown .... April and often May.
9. Light Snipe .... Middle of April to middle of May and again in September.
10. Dark Needle .... Middle of April to end of June and again in September.
11. Brown Owl .... Latter part of April to end of June.
12. Olive Bloa .... Latter part of April and throughout May.
13. Dark Watchet .... Last week in April and throughout May and sometimes early June.
14. Yellow Partridge ...... May to middle of June.
15. Light Needle .... May, June and July.
16. Yellow-Legged Bloa .. May to end of June.
17. Dotterel .... Middle of May to end of Season.
18. Poult Bloa .... Middle of May to middle of July.
19. Gravel Bed .... Middle of May to end of June.
20. Stone Midge .... Middle of May to end of June.
21. Knotted Midge ...... Middle of May to end of July.
22. Black Gnat .... Middle of May to end of August.
23. Ginger Spinner (Wet) .. June, July and August.

24. Dark Sedge   ....   Middle of June to the end of the
                              Season.
25. Light Sedge ....   Middle of June to the end of the
                              Season.
26. Red Spinner (Wet) ....   July, August and September.
27. July Dun ....   July and August.
28. Rough-Bodied Poult ..   July, August and September.
29. Pale Watery Dun......   Middle of July to the end of Septem-
                              ber.
30. Light Silverhorns ....   Middle of July to the end of August.
31. Dark Silverhorns ......   Middle of July to the end of August.
32. August Dun   ....   Last week in July, August and
                              September.
33. Ant ....   August to second week in September
34. Green Insect ....   August and September.
35. Ginger Spinner (Dry) ..   June, July and August.
36. Red Spinner (Dry) ....   July, August and September.

TABLE II.

MARCH.	APRIL.
Winter Brown.	Winter Brown.
Waterhen Bloa.	Waterhen Bloa.
Greenwell's Glory.	Greenwell's Glory.
Spring Black.	Spring Black.
Dark Snipe.	Dark Snipe.
Orange Partridge.	Orange Partridge.
Broughton's Point.	Broughton's Point.
	March Brown.
	Light Snipe.
	Dark Needle.
	Brown Owl.
	Olive Bloa.
	Dark Watchet.

MAY.
Greenwell's Glory.
Orange Partridge.
March Brown.
Light Snipe.
Dark Needle.
Brown Owl.
Olive Bloa.
Dark Watchet.
Yellow Partridge.
Light Needle.
Yellow-Legged Bloa.
Dotterel.
Poult Bloa.
Gravel Bed.
Stone Midge.
Knotted Midge.
Black Gnat.

JUNE.
Dark Needle.
Brown Owl.
Dark Watchet.
Yellow Partridge.
Light Needle.
Yellow-Legged Bloa.
Dotterel.
Poult Bloa.
Gravel Bed.
Stone Midge.
Knotted Midge.
Black Gnat.
Ginger Spinner (Wet and Dry).
Dark Sedge.
Light Sedge.

JULY.
Light Needle.
Dotterel.
Poult Bloa.
Knotted Midge.
Black Gnat.
Ginger Spinner
    (Wet and Dry).
Dark Sedge.
Light Sedge.
Red Spinner
    (Wet and Dry).
July Dun.
Rough-Bodied Poult.
Pale Watery Dun.
Light Silverhorns.
Dark Silverhorns.
August Dun.

AUGUST.
Dotterel.
Black Gnat.
Ginger Spinner
    (Wet and Dry).
Dark Sedge.
Light Sedge.
Red Spinner
    (Wet and Dry).
July Dun.
Rough-bodied Poult.
Pale Watery Dun.
Light Silverhorns.
Dark Silverhorns.
August Dun.
Ant.
Green Insect.

SEPTEMBER.
Waterhen Bloa.
Greenwell's Glory.
Dark Snipe.
Light Snipe.
Dark Needle.
Dotterel.
Dark Sedge.
Light Sedge.
Red Spinner.
    (Wet and Dry).
Rough-Bodied Poult.
Pale Watery Dun.
August Dun
Ant.
Green Insect.

DRESSINGS.

WET FLIES.

No. 1.

WINTER BROWN.

PERLIDÆ.

Hook 1 or 2.

WINGS.—Hackled with a greyish feather, barred, from the under coverts of a Woodcock's wing. (The lighter side of the feather towards the head of the fly).

BODY.—Orange silk, No. 6a, dubbed with ruddy brown wool, the three turns next the tail showing distinct orange.

HEAD.—Bronze Peacock herl.

March to middle of April.

No. 2.

WATERHEN BLOA,

EPHEMERIDÆ.

Hook 1 or 2.

WINGS.—Hackled with a smoky grey feather from the under coverts of a Waterhen's wing. (The darker side of the feather towards the head of the fly).

BODY.—Yellow silk, No. 4, dubbed with Mole's fur.

HEAD.—Yellow silk.

March to end of April, and again in September.

No. 3.

GREENWELL'S GLORY.

EPHEMERIDÆ.

Hook 1 or 2.

WINGS.—From a hen Blackbird's primary quill feather, bunched and split.

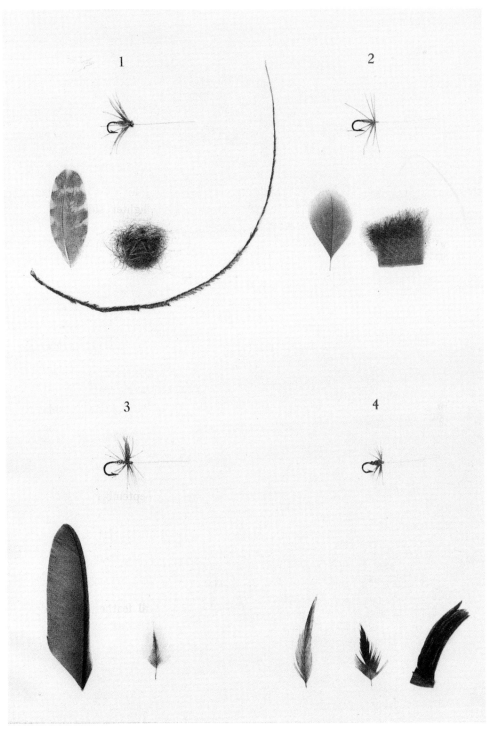

BODY.—Yellow silk, No. 4, well waxed, ribbed with four turns of fine gold wire or tinsel.

LEGS.—Cochybondu Hen's hackle.

HEAD.—Yellow silk, well waxed.

March to first week in May, and again in September, although, by dressing with a lighter wing, body and hackle, the fly can be used during the intervening months.

No. 4.
SPRING BLACK.
DIPTERA (GNAT).
Hook 0.

WINGS.—Hackled with a black Cock's hackle or a blue black feather from an adult Starling's neck.

BODY.—Purple silk, No. 8, dubbed sparingly with Magpie herl.

HEAD.—Purple silk.

March and early April.

No. 5.
DARK SNIPE OR SNIPE AND PURPLE.
EPHEMERIDÆ.
Hook 1.

WINGS.—Hackled with the dark feather from the marginal coverts of a Snipe's wing.

BODY.—Purple silk, No. 8.

HEAD.—Purple silk.

March to middle of April, and again in September.

No. 6.
ORANGE PARTRIDGE.
PERLIDÆ AND EPHEMERIDÆ.
Hook 1.

WINGS.—Hackled with a brown mottled (not barred) feather from a Partridge's neck, or back.

BODY.—Orange silk, No. 6a, or orange silk, No. 6a, ribbed with about four turns of gold wire or tinsel.

HEAD.—Orange silk.

March to middle of May.

No. 7.

BROUGHTON'S POINT OR DARK BLOA.

EPHEMERIDÆ.

Hook 1 or 2.

WINGS.—From a Starling's primary quill feather, the outer side of the feather as the under side of the wing.

BODY.—Claret silk, No. 13.

LEGS.—A black Hen's hackle.

HEAD.—Claret silk.

March to middle of April.

No. 8a.

MARCH BROWN.

EPHEMERIDÆ.

Hook 2 or 3.

WINGS.—From a quill feather from a Partridge's tail, greyish in tone, the top side of the feather as the under side of the wing.

BODY.—Orange silk, No. 6a, dubbed with sandy fur taken from near the base of a Hare's ear and ribbed with yellow silk, No. 4.

TAIL.—Two strands from a Partridge's tail, same feather as the one used for the wings.

LEGS.—Greyish brown feather from a Partridge's back.

HEAD.—Orange silk.

April and often May.

5

6

7

8A

No. 8b.
MARCH BROWN.
EPHEMERIDÆ.
Hook 2 or 3.

WINGS.—Hackled with a mottled brown feather from a Snipe's rump.

BODY.—Orange silk, No. 6a, dubbed with fur from the nape of a Rabbit's neck which has been lightly tinged red with Crawshaw's Red Spinner dye, and ribbed with gold wire or tinsel.

TAIL.—Two strands from a feather from a Snipe's rump, same feather as is used for the wings.

HEAD.—Orange silk.

April, and often May.

No. 9.
LIGHT SNIPE OR SNIPE BLOA.
EPHEMERIDÆ.
Hook 1.

WINGS.—Hackled with a bluish feather from the under coverts of a Snipe's wing. (The lighter side of the feather towards the head of the fly).

BODY.—Yellow silk, No. 4.

HEAD.—Yellow silk.

Middle of April to middle of May, and again in September.

No. 10.
DARK NEEDLE.
PERLIDÆ.
Hook 1.

WINGS.—Hackled with a brownish feather taken from where the hinder part of a Starling's wing joins the body, (There are only about four of these feathers on each side of the bird.) or with a brownish feather from the back of a Swift.

BODY.—Orange brown silk, No. 6b.

HEAD.—Magpie herl.

Middle of April to the end of June, and again in September.

No. 11.
BROWN OWL.
TRICHOPTERA.
Hook 1.

WINGS.—Hackled with a reddish brown feather from the lesser coverts of a Tawny or Brown Owl's wing.

BODY.—Orange silk, No. 6a.

HEAD.—Bronze Peacock herl.

Latter part of April to end of June.

No. 12.
OLIVE BLOA.
EPHEMERIDÆ.
Hook 1.

WINGS.—Hackled with an olive green feather from a Green Plover's neck.

BODY.—Yellow silk, No. 4, well waxed.

HEAD.—Orange brown silk, No. 6b.

Latter part of April and throughout May.

No. 13a.
DARK WATCHET OR IRON BLUE DUN.
EPHEMERIDÆ.
Hook 0 or 00.

WINGS.—Hackled with a dark smoky blue feather from a Jackdaw's throat.

BODY.—Orange and purple silk, Nos. 6a and 8, twisted together, dubbed very sparingly with Mole's fur and wound on the body so that the orange and purple show in alternate bands.

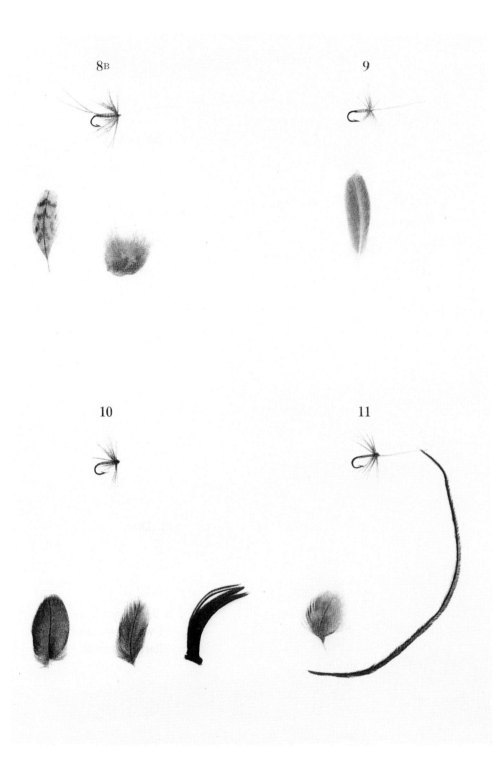

12

13A

13B

14

HEAD.—Orange silk.

Last week in April and throughout May, and sometimes early June. Particularly for dull days.

No. 13b.
DARK WATCHET OR IRON BLUE DUN.
EPHEMERIDÆ.
Hook 0 or 00.

WINGS.—From the darkish blue feather from a Blue Tit's tail, bunched and split.

BODY.—Same as No. 13a.

TAIL.—Two strands from a medium grizzled blue Cock's hackle.

LEGS.—Feather from a young Starling's thigh or flank.

HEAD.—Orange silk.

Last week in April and throughout May, and sometimes early June. For brighter days.

No. 14.
YELLOW PARTRIDGE.
PERLIDÆ AND DIPTERA (Crane-fly).
Hook 0 or 1.

WINGS.—Hackled with a greyish feather barely tinged with brown, from a Partridge's back.

BODY.—Yellow silk, No. 4.

HEAD.—Yellow silk.

May to middle of June.

No. 15.
LIGHT NEEDLE.
PERLIDÆ.
Hook 0 or 1.

WINGS.—Hackled with a feather from a young Starling's thigh or flank.

BODY.—Orange silk, No. 6a.

HEAD.—Orange silk.

May, June and July.

No. 16.

YELLOW-LEGGED BLOA.
EPHEMERIDÆ.
Hook 1.

WINGS.—From a young Starling's light primary quill feather, the outer side of the feather as the under side of the wing.

BODY.—Primrose yellow silk, No. 3.

TAIL.—Two strands from a very pale ginger Cock's hackle.

LEGS.—A Cock's hackle dyed a rich primrose yellow.

HEAD.—Primrose yellow silk.

May to end of June.

No. 17.

DOTTEREL.
EPHEMERIDÆ.
Hook 1.

WINGS.—Hackled with a light-tipped fawnish feather from the marginal coverts or lesser coverts of a Dotterel's wing.

BODY.—Orange silk, No. 6, or primrose yellow silk, No. 3.

HEAD.—Orange silk, or primrose yellow silk.

If the Dotterel feather is unobtainable a feather from the under coverts of a young Starling's wing makes a fair substitute.

Middle of May to end of Season.

No. 18.

POULT BLOA.
EPHEMERIDÆ.
Hook 0 or 1.

WINGS.—Hackled with a light blue feather from the under coverts of a young Grouse wing, taken before the bird is strong on the wing. (The lighter side of the feather towards the head of the fly.) This feather darkens very rapidly on the live bird from August onwards.

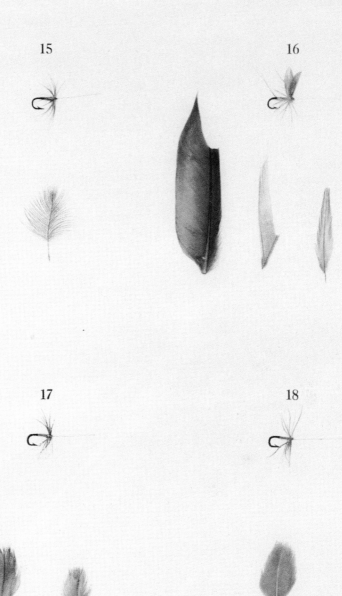

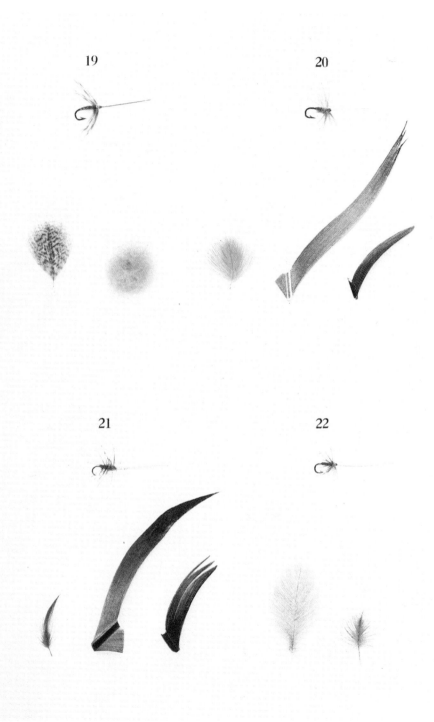

BODY.—Primrose yellow silk, No. 3.

HEAD.—Primrose yellow silk.

Middle of May to middle of July.

No. 19.
GRAVEL BED.
DIPTERA (Crane-fly).
Hook 1.

WINGS.—Hackled with a greyish feather, lightly tinged with brown, from a Partridge's neck.

BODY.—Blue silk, No. 7, dubbed with blue-grey fur from the flank of an Opossum.

HEAD.—Blue silk.

Middle of May to end of June. A useful fly in a coloured water.

No. 20.
STONE MIDGE.
DIPTERA (Gnat).
Hook 0 or 00.

WINGS.—Hackled with an olive green feather from a Green Plover's neck.

BODY.—Grey silk, No. 9a, well waxed, or ash-coloured silk, No. 10, but in both cases dubbed sparingly with bluey-grey Heron herl.

HEAD.—Magpie herl.

Middle of May to end of June.

No. 21.
KNOTTED MIDGE.
DIPTERA (Gnat).
Hook 0 or 00.

WINGS.—Hackled down the body "palmerwise" with a small black Cock's hackle.

BODY.—Ash-coloured silk, No. 10, dubbed with dark Heron herl.
HEAD.—Magpie herl.

Middle of May to end of July.

For close days.

——————

No. 22.

BLACK GNAT.

DIPTERA (Gnat).

Hook 00.

WINGS.—A few fibres from a light blue Hen's hackle put on as a single wing.
BODY.—Black silk, No. 9.
LEGS.—Rusty black Hen's hackle.
HEAD.—Black silk.

Middle of May to end of August.

For close days.

——————

No. 23.

GINGER SPINNER.

EPHEMERIDÆ.

Hook 0 or 1.

WINGS.—Fibres of light grizzled blue Cock's hackle.
BODY.—Flat gold wire with a wrapping over it of orange silk, No. 6, the silk to be untwisted and only one or two strands used.
TAIL.—Two strands from a ginger Cock's hackle.
LEGS.—Ginger Cock's hackle.
HEAD.—Orange silk.

June, July and August.

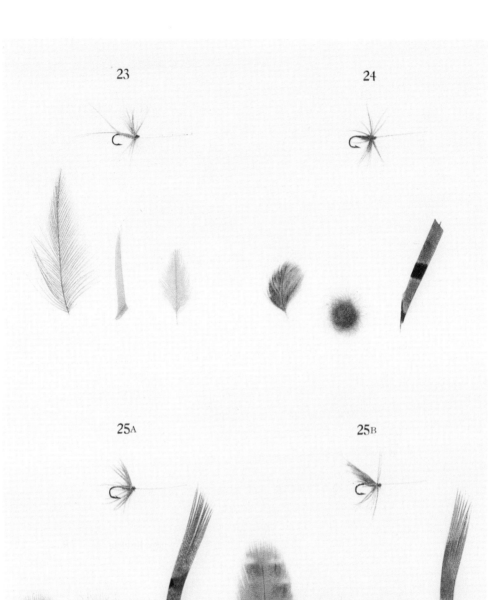

No. 24.

DARK SEDGE.

TRICHOPTERA.

Hook 1 or 2.

WINGS.—Hackled with a reddish brown feather from the lesser coverts of a Tawny or Brown Owl's wing.

BODY.—Yellow silk, No. 4, dubbed with brownish fawn Seal's fur.

HEAD.—Brownish green herl from the tail of a cock Pheasant.

Middle of June to end of the Season.

No. 25a.

LIGHT SEDGE.

TRICHOPTERA.

Hook 1 or 2.

WINGS.—Hackled with a light-barred reddish feather, from the lesser coverts of a Landrail's wing.

BODY.—Yellow silk, No. 4, dubbed with reddish fur from the thigh of a Squirrel.

HEAD.—A reddish herl from the tail of a cock Pheasant.

Middle of June to the end of the Season.

No. 25b.

LIGHT SEDGE.

TRICHOPTERA.

Hook 1 or 2.

WINGS.—From a light barred reddish feather, from the lesser coverts of a Landrail's wing (a larger feather than the one used for No. 25a), the outer side of the feather as the outside of the wing. Wings put on " penthouse " fashion.

BODY.—Same as No. 25a.

LEGS.—Reddish feather from the marginal coverts of a Landrail's wing.

HEAD.—Same as No. 25a.

Middle of June to the end of the Season.

No. 26.

RED SPINNER.

EPHEMERIDÆ.

Hook 1.

WINGS.—Fibres of medium grizzled blue Cock's hackle.

BODY.—Red silk, No. 12, dubbed with maroon wool and ribbed with four turns of fine gold wire or tinsel.

TAIL.—Two strands from a deep red Cock's hackle.

LEGS.—Deep red Cock's hackle.

HEAD.—Red silk.

July, August and September.

No. 27.

JULY DUN.

EPHEMERIDÆ.

Hook 1.

WINGS.—From a Coot's primary quill feather, the outer side of the feather as the under side of the wing.

BODY.—Yellow silk, No. 4, dubbed sparingly with Mole's fur.

TAIL.—Two strands from a medium olive Cock's hackle.

LEGS.—Medium olive Hen's hackle.

HEAD.—Yellow silk.

July and August.

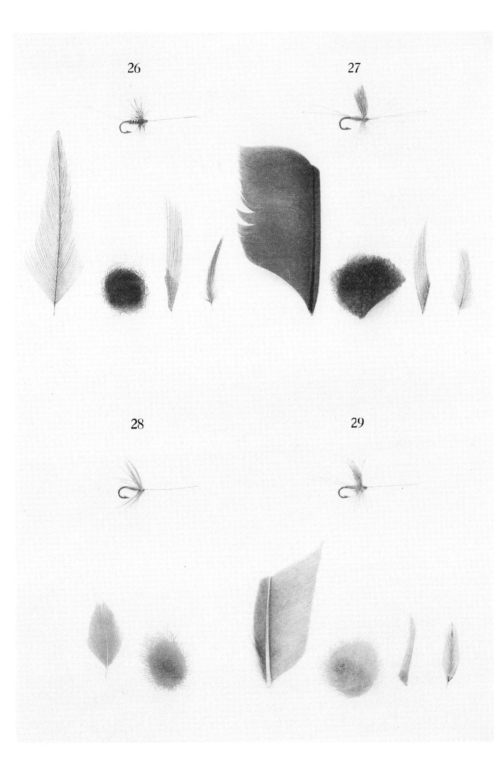

No. 28.
ROUGH-BODIED POULT.
EPHEMERIDÆ.
Hook 0 or 1.

WINGS.—Hackled with a light blue feather from the under coverts of a young Grouse wing, taken before the bird is strong on the wing. (The lighter side of the feather towards the head of the fly.) This feather darkens very rapidly on the live bird from August onwards.

BODY.—Straw-coloured silk, No. 2, dubbed sparingly with buff fur from the flank of an Opossum.

HEAD.—Straw-coloured silk.

July, August and September.

No. 29.
PALE WATERY DUN.
EPHEMERIDÆ.
Hook 0 or 1.

WINGS.—From a young Starling's light primary quill feather, the inner side of the feather as the under side of the wing.

BODY.—Yellow silk, No. 4, dubbed with palest buff fur from the flank of an Oppossum.

TAIL.—Two strands from palest ginger Cock's hackle.

LEGS.—Light blue Hen's hackle.

HEAD.—Yellow silk.

Middle of July to the end of September.

No. 30.
LIGHT SILVERHORNS.
TRICHOPTERA.
Hook 1.

WINGS.—From a Thrush's secondary quill feather, the outer side of the feather as the outside of the wing, or from a Landrail's primary quill feather, the outer side of the feather as the outside of the wing. Wings put on " penthouse " fashion.

BODY.—Ash-coloured silk, No. 10, sparingly dubbed with reddish grey fur from the thigh of a Squirrel.

LEGS.—Feather from a young Starling's thigh or flank.

HEAD.—Ash-coloured silk.

ANTENNÆ.—Two strands from a black and white feather from a Mallard's breast.

Middle of July to the end of August.

No. 31.
DARK SILVERHORNS.
TRICHOPTERA.
Hook 1.

WINGS.—From a Waterhen's primary quill feather, the outer side of the feather as the outside of the wing. Wings put on " penthouse " fashion.

BODY.—Black silk, No. 9, dubbed very sparingly with Mole's fur and ribbed with olive silk, No. 11.

LEGS.—Black Cock's hackle or Green Plover's topping.

HEAD.—Black silk.

ANTENNÆ.—Two strands from a black and white feather from a Mallard's breast.

Middle of July to the end of August.

No. 32.
AUGUST DUN.
EPHEMERIDÆ.
Hook 2.

WINGS.—From a Mallard's breast feather, lightly tinged with brown.

BODY.—Yellow silk, No. 4, dubbed with yellow olive wool and

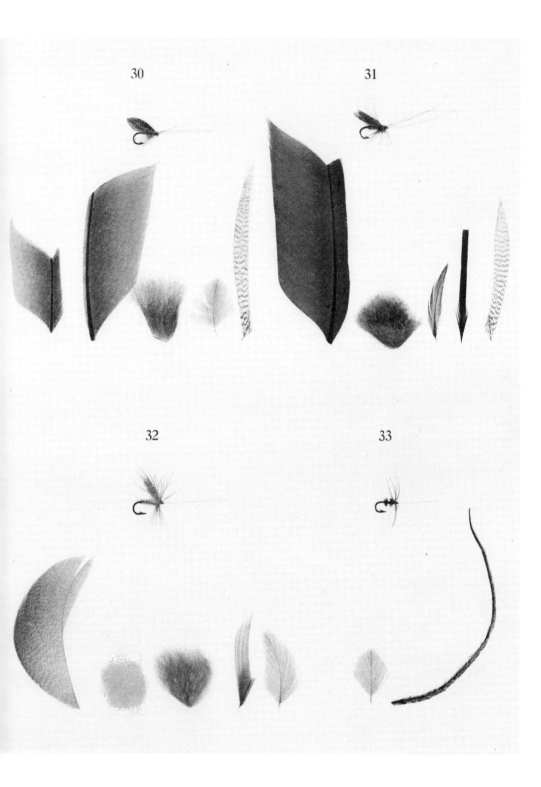

ribbed with orange silk, No. 6, sparingly spun with fur from the nape of a Rabbit's neck which has been lightly tinged red with Crawshaw's Red Spinner dye.

TAIL.—Two strands from a medium olive Cock's hackle.

LEGS.—Medium olive Hen's hackle.

HEAD.—Yellow silk.

Last week in July, August and September.

No. 33.

ANT.

HYMENOPTERA.

Hook 0.

WINGS.—Hackled with a light blue Hen's hackle.

BODY.—Orange brown silk, No. 6b, dressed full at the tail with bronze Peacock herl, then a few turns of the silk towards the head, then dressed full at the shoulder with bronze Peacock herl.

HEAD.—Orange brown silk.

August to second week in September.

No. 34.

GREEN INSECT.

APHIDES.

Hook 00 or 000.

WINGS.—Hackled with a light blue Cock's hackle.

BODY.—Yellow silk, No. 4, dubbed with bright green olive wool.

HEAD.—Yellow silk.

August and September.   Particularly on gusty days.

DRY FLIES.
No. 35.
GINGER SPINNER.
EPHEMERIDÆ.
Hook 0 or 1, eyed.

WINGS.—Fibres of light grizzled blue Cock's hackle dressed " spent."

BODY.—Light cinnamon quill.

TAIL.—Two strands from a ginger Cock's hackle.

LEGS.—Ginger Cock's hackle, two turns at the most, as the fly must be dressed lightly.

HEAD.—Orange silk, No. 6.

June, July and August.

No. 36.
RED SPINNER.
EPHEMERIDÆ.
Hook 0 or 1, eyed.

WINGS.—Fibres of medium grizzled blue Cock's hackle dressed " spent."

BODY.—Red quill.

TAIL.—Two strands of Gallina, dyed red brown.

LEGS.—Deep red Cock's hackle, two turns at the most, as the fly must be dressed lightly.

HEAD.—Red silk, No. 12.

July, August and September.

34

35

36

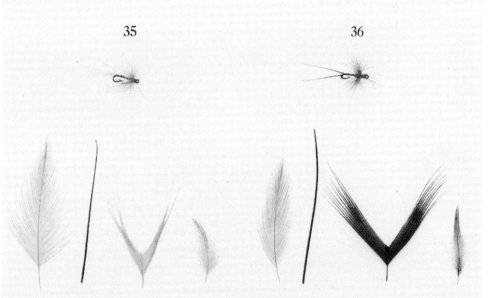

A Typical Stretch

Photo by
Mrs. A. R. Gurney

Chapter II.

FLY FISHING.

SO much has already been written on fly fishing by men of wide and varied experience, that it is with no little diffidence the writers approach the subject. Yet the more thoroughly the whole art of trout fishing is explored, the more engrossing does it become, and, as experience is gained, the more evident it appears that little is really known and that a vast field still remains open for investigation.

It is not intended to try in this chapter to teach the art of fly fishing, as more can be learned by observation, perseverance and practice on the river, than by reading all that was ever written on the subject ; but it is desired, by emphasizing a few essential points, to help the novice through his initial difficulties.

Some anglers who are only able to devote a few weeks during the season to their pastime are content to go to the local tackle dealer or the professional fisherman and to rely entirely on his advice. While it is always well to consult the " local men" —quaint

characters for the most part and many of them cobblers
by trade—it is often a mistake to rely entirely upon
them ; for, if a man's ambition be to get out of the
rut and to kill fish under difficult conditions, he must
think for himself.

The " local man " often has a strong partiality for
certain patterns of flies, no matter what the conditions.
Only recently the writers came across a most glaring
example of this particular tendency, which is perhaps
worth mentioning in order to illustrate their point.
Arriving at the river one September afternoon, they
noticed on the opposite bank the local professional,
who is held in very high esteem as a fisherman. He
certainly casts as neat a line as the writers have ever
seen thrown. In answer to their enquiry, " What
sport ?", they received the reply, " A few," and were
more than a little astonished to learn that he was
using flies which, in their opinion, were more suitable
for the end of July. It is always a pleasure to see this
man cast, so they sat down and watched him. Time
after time he put his flies in the most beautiful manner
over rising fish, but without result, although the water
was coloured and the fish continued to rise steadily.
Soon one showed within casting distance of the bank on
which the writers were seated, so a fly was immediately
put over him and was accepted at the first offer.
Earlier that day there had been a large hatch of Dark
Needles, and it was an imitation of that insect which

induced the rise. Alternately the writers threw over rising fish with more or less success; but the professional, who persevered for another half-hour without changing his flies, at last gave up in disgust. For the time being at least he was beaten. Not that he did not know the river or understand the habits of the trout—both were to him as an open book—but simply because he was deficient in his knowledge of insect life. This man probably knew some ten or a dozen good all-round flies which he used the season through, but without due regard to the hatch of natural insects.

Now put yourself in the professional's position on that particular day, only add to his knowledge that of insect life. On finding your flies rejected, you would have picked from off the water, and examined, the natural insects which were floating down; then, immediately realizing what was amiss, you would have substituted an imitation of the taking fly for one on your cast. Success would have followed failure, and a light-hearted angler would have tramped homewards at sunset with a creel the heavier for his practical knowledge.

From the foregoing it will be gathered that the novice should make it his first duty to study on every possible occasion the insect life of the river he is going to fish, and not merely rely upon the tackle dealer or professional to supply his deficiency in this, or indeed in other matters. By this let it not be thought that the writers consider it necessary to go deeply into the study of entomology, fascinating as that study is ; but if the greatest amount of pleasure is to be derived, and incidentally a fair number of fish to be killed, it is essential that the angler should arm himself with a good general knowledge of river insect life.

A great deal in this direction can be learned by an occasional emptying of a trout's stomach into a glass of water, and an examination of the *débris* after they have been separated by a brisk stir round.   It is most instructive, and it shows how catholic fish are in their feeding.   It shows too, not infrequently, the reasons for a poor day's sport, and often gives a hint which may turn failure into success on some future occasion.

Though a knowledge of insect life is highly important, it is equally necessary to learn to adapt oneself to varying conditions.

This latter point may at the first glance appear unnecessarily elementary, so much so as to seem hardly worth making, but speaking from personal experience, the writers think that, probably on account of its very obviousness, it often receives far less attention than it deserves.

How many anglers, after working the long winter through begin, as the trout season draws near, to let their thoughts wander to some favourite stream and live for days, aye, almost weeks, in anticipation of the opening day ? They conjure up in their minds all the

details that have gone to make up some red-letter day
in the past, the whole scene comes up as fresh as
ever, and memory, ever willing, gives them a most
vivid picture of the pool in which the fish of the
season put up his last gallant struggle. They recall
those exciting moments when the strength of the cast
was taxed to its utmost as the fish wildly endeavoured
to reach the roots of an overhanging tree, and the
joyful feeling of power that crept over them when at
last the lusty trout, having somewhat spent himself,
allowed them to regain a foot or two of line. Then
came that last mad rush when the captive perceived
the net.

These memories are happy indeed, though often
enough they lead one astray, as, when the eve of the
opening day arrives, one has probably definitely
decided to begin operations at the exact pool that was
the scene of one's former success. Is this adapting
oneself to circumstances ? It can hardly be so, and
yet probably very few can say that they have never
fallen a victim to such foolishness.

The wise man waits until the morrow, when he can
see how the wind strikes his favourite stream or reach,
whether the water is too high or too low, and whether
the sport that it normally might be expected to yield
is going to be adversely affected by any other condition. If so, even though disappointed, he will find
a more suitable place at which to begin and no doubt

at the end of the day his creel will reveal the reward of his adaptability to circumstance.

The consideration of adaptability to circumstance naturally brings one to a classification and subsequent subdivision of the methods of fly fishing, which methods, judiciously and intelligently combined, make for the true road to success.

Fly fishing may be practised in two principal ways, with the wet fly and with the dry fly.

In the former, as the name implies, the flies are fished slightly submerged ; and three or sometimes four flies may be used on the cast. They are placed some 20 inches or so apart, but varied as to distance according to the state of the river, greater distance between them being necessary, and fewer flies being used, in low clear water. In dry-fly fishing, as perhaps it is unnecessary to state, only one fly is used, and it is made to float by being whipped through the air after each cast, so as to shake off any globules of water that may be attached to the feathers, a process which is generally assisted by the fly being lightly touched with oil before use.

Before going further it is as well to say a few words regarding the rod and tackle. The length of rod the writers find most useful is 10 ft. 6 ins., and, if it is to be used for wet-fly fishing exclusively, they would unhesitatingly recommend a two-piece rod made of greenheart, or of hickory for the butt, with greenheart

top, not too whippy and not too stiff. Such a rod is
softer in the action and less tiring to the wrist than
one made of split cane. That is a matter well worth
consideration when one is whipping the stream for
long periods at a stretch.

For dry-fly fishing however, and general use, and
for almost unending wear, a split-cane rod by one of
the first-class makers will probably best suit the
requirements of the average man ; only in selecting
the rod, of whatever pattern, great care should be
devoted to getting one which, with reel and line
attached, will make a harmonious whole. If the rod
be a split cane, it should be rather more whippy than
the average type in use on Chalk streams. These
points should be carefully attended to, otherwise the
beginner, after working for an hour or so, will find
his wrist growing tired, and he will then get into a
slovenly way of casting, which is easier to learn than
to unlearn.

Regarding the reel, line and cast, we should recommend, if the reader is buying his rod from a man of
practical experience, that he leaves the first two to
the maker's discretion. He will then no doubt get
both reel and line of suitable weight for the rod. The
cast should be approximately three yards, tapered,
the last yard being of finest drawn gut for ordinary
waters, but a coarser cast may be used when fishing
a full or slightly coloured water. A good cast for

ordinary waters can be made of ten strands of gut, each strand either 12 or 14 inches in length and tapered as follows :—First two strands of Quarter drawn, then two strands of Half drawn, then three strands of 2x, and finally three strands of 4x.

WET-FLY FISHING.

It is with wet-fly fishing that it is proposed to deal first, as this method is by far the more important on the majority of North Country rivers, the dry fly being a useful auxiliary under conditions to be detailed later.

Why, it may be asked, should the fish be more partial to the wet fly than to the dry fly on Northern streams. The reason is not far to seek; for, owing to the roughness and rapidity of such rivers, a large percentage of insects, as they rise from the bed of the river preparatory to hatching out, are carried many yards downstream before they reach the surface of the water. Others, getting into rough water, find themselves unequal to the effort of emerging from their nymphal case, or emerge with wetted and helpless wings, while many flies, surviving these natural difficulties, are carried down some rapid almost immediately after they reach the perfect state, and get water-logged before ever they have the opportunity of using their wings. Hence the trout become used to taking much of their insect food in a submerged or partially submerged state. Therefore so long as those streams remain as heretofore, the wet fly is likely to continue to hold the premier position in the filling of a North Countryman's creel.

There are two methods of fishing the wet fly, upstream and downstream. Follows an attempt to give a brief outline of how and when each method may be used to the best advantage.

The use of the word "downstream" in this connection is, perhaps, somewhat misleading, for it is not intended to refer to that method of fishing in which the angler casts his flies across and downstream, allowing the current to sweep them round to a point below him, in the same manner as when fishing the salmon fly. To fish an imitation of a natural insect in such a way as to make it resist the onward flow of the water in a most unnatural manner, is, in the writers' judgment, unsound, and they wish it to be understood that, by "downstream," they do not allude to this manner of fishing.

The downstream method advocated might quite appropriately be termed across-stream fishing, as the angler faces the bank towards which he purposes fishing, casts across and slightly upstream, then allows the flies to be carried without drag till they reach a point a few yards below where they alighted upon the water. Wading downstream a yard or more, he repeats the cast, until the whole stream has been worked in this manner. The only reason for the term

" downstream " being used in connection with this class of fishing is that the angler himself works down the river.

The next question for consideration is, when is downstream fishing advisable ? It may truly be answered, " Not often," for its practice might be confined to strong and full waters, to waters tinged with colour, to cold Spring days before and after the hatch, to evening fishing in such places as have the river flowing towards the sunset, and, lastly, to occasions when a heavy downstream wind or the nature of the country leaves the angler no choice.

The enthusiast frequently finds himself on the river bank on a Spring morning long before the sun's rays have warmed the air, or any sign of insect life is visible. With experience he will find that at such times the trout are not in the heavy rapid streams, but may be looked for in steady flowing water.

A favourite place, which the writers would never pass by on such an occasion, is formed when a stream some two feet deep flows gently along the edge of a bank, and particularly if the bank be overhung, or other natural causes make it a harbour or refuge for the stream's inhabitants.

Let the novice who finds himself, cold Spring weather prevailing, at the top of such a stream, cast in the manner described across, but slightly upstream, towards such bank. As the flies are carried down, let him vibrate the point of his rod slightly by an up and down motion in order to make his flies appear as though they were struggling to reach the surface of the water. Ten to one before the stream is fished out a sharp pluck will be felt, but the beginner, unprepared, will in many cases leave his fly in the fish or miss him altogether. The hooking of trout under such conditions is difficult in the extreme, as frequently no rise is seen ; and it is only by perseverance, leading to appreciation of the moment to strike, that he can hope to succeed.

To teach in theory the correct method and timing of the strike under such conditions, is beyond the writers. The knowledge seems to come to the persevering almost as a sixth sense. At times it is positively uncanny to watch an " artist," in his instinctive response to the rises of fish under the conditions described, for they are totally invisible to the average man.

Practice, coupled with intelligent reasoning out of the whys and wherefores of success and failure, will do more to help the novice than anything else. But, even with the rod in the hands of a past-master, this method of downstream fishing will not always succeed, though the waiting hour before the rise may often be well spent in giving these tactics a trial.

As soon, however, as the first insects floating on the surface have been noticed by the fish, the time has come to change methods and to fish upstream.

Upstream fishing is far more difficult than down-stream fishing, and the initial efforts will prove disheartening. Rise after rise will be missed, and the flies will be swept to the feet of the angler almost before he has seen where they lit. It is nevertheless all important that the novice should school himself in this branch of fly fishing beyond any other, as upon it will depend his future success.

The education of the angler who has only mastered downstream fishing, or even dry-fly fishing, is incomplete ; and, though the dry-fly purist may shrug his shoulders at the remark, it is not too much to say that, if he were transferred from the pellucid waters of the Chalk stream to some rapid broken river of the North, and were to endeavour to fish the wet fly, it would be some considerable time before he achieved any great success. Whereas the man who has once thoroughly mastered the art of fishing the wet fly *upstream* would be able quickly to adapt himself to the conditions and surroundings of the home of the dry fly.

Scoffers have often termed wet-fly fishing in general the "chuck and chance it" method, but those who thus described it can never have seen an expert at work fishing upstream. There is no such thing as "chuck and chance it" in the way he throws his flies. Every cast is made to a definite point, not necessarily to a rising fish, as in dry-fly fishing, but successively to each of the many little runs, eddies, channels, and slack waters behind boulders, which his experience teaches are likely to hold feeding fish. It is just the experience gained by such definite fishing that the dry-fly purist who throws to none but feeding fish would lack, if he overcame his prejudices and essayed to throw the wet fly on Northern waters.

The obvious natural law which causes fish to lie head upstream should convince the reader that no undue stress has been laid upon the importance of fishing upstream, and that that method should be rigidly adhered to on all occasions, except those previously mentioned.

That trout have exceptionally keen eyesight, no one who has ever walked along the banks of a trout stream will deny. How then can the least thoughtful expect to creel decent fish with the river in normal condition, if he stands with the fish below him, or, for that matter, stands anywhere within their very wide range of vision, a range so wide that, if a circle be described with the head of a trout for the centre, only about one-sixth of the circumference of such a circle, and that immediately behind, would appear to be outside the range of vision of the fish?

From these well-known facts it will be obvious, even to the uninitiated, that the best approach for the angler bent on capturing trout in clear water is from behind. Yet, astonishing as it may seem (and for the

simple reason that it is the easier way), many men—
we might almost say the majority of men—invariably
fish their flies across and downstream, letting the
flies sweep right round until they are directly below,
where they are often allowed to dangle in the water
at the end of a taut line.

To fish downstream in this manner requires no particular skill, as the stream does most of the work ;
and, while the great majority of fish risen are merely
pricked and lost, those caught are below the average
of size for the river fished. If the beginner is having
a bad day and everything is going wrong, if he grows
tired with his efforts to fish upstream and is tempted
to resort to this method, rather than do so, let him
knock off for a while and smoke a pipe, and then return,
with renewed hope and vigour, to his upstream fishing,
determined to master it.

Now it frequently happens that the angler wading
upstream gets almost up to, or at any rate within two
or three yards of a fish, before ever his presence is
noticed. There is therefore in general little necessity
to use a long line when fishing upstream, yet it is often
done.

Frequently anglers are met who say that they cannot
fish upstream, urging, by way of excuse, that they have
difficulty in seeing fish rise, which causes late striking,
the fish being missed entirely, or, at the most, only
turned over. Of course it is difficult to see a rise, or

to strike a fish, in a rapid stream if a long line is used, and in the majority of these cases the reason for failure is to be found in the use of too long a line.

Therefore the novice who is bent on mastering fly-fishing upstream can almost dismiss from his mind *the first part* of the " far off and fine " theory. In practice it will be found that, for fishing strong flowing streams, a line (including the cast) but little longer than the rod is ample ; while for fishing the more gently flowing shallow water at the edges of such streams, another yard or two of line will be necessary to assist the angler in keeping out of sight. The angler must be ruled by circumstances, always bearing in mind the fact that the most practical length of line to use is the shortest on which a trout may be killed. Once this fact has been fully appreciated and carried into practice, many of the supposed difficulties of upstream fishing will vanish entirely, leaving the novice free to tackle other problems.

Arriving at a likely stretch of water, and full of excitement on noticing a fish rise at the tail of the main stream, the beginner will often wade straight out to a point below the fish and then cast over him. There is always a temptation, even to the expert, to go for a rising fish, but under such circumstances, if the angler be wise, he will take a careful survey before wading out, and will note the character of the water within casting distance of the edge.

The experienced angler will do this instinctively, and will make his first cast to the sharp run at the edge of the bank. His second will be made slightly more across ; and, after he has released another foot or two of line, his flies at the third throw will search the slack water behind the rock. Here the cast will be repeated two or three times in rapid succession, the flies not being allowed to remain in the water more than a moment, lest the current pick up the line and cause a drag.

The fear of drag is ever present, but drag may be avoided in many cases, if care is exercised in regulating the speed at which the rod point is raised as the flies are swept down by the current. When the flies have been thrown to a quieter bit of water and there is a danger of the current picking up the line, the moment of drag can often be postponed if the cast finishes in a wavy line on the water, as the current has to pick up the slack before the drag takes effect on the flies. To cast thus is a feat not difficult of achievement for many of the fraternity.

Another throw is now made, then another, each rather more across stream, and then, as a result of the next cast, the flies are hustled rapidly down a race between two boulders. Here, as in all swift-flowing water, it is necessary to make several casts before the angler can be sure that his flies have thoroughly searched the run ; and it is most important to keep in mind that the casts of a past master at upstream fly fishing follow quickly one after another.

Headwaters of the Aire

Photo by   N.W. Lee

Wading now a few yards across stream, the angler continues this system of casting until he eventually reaches a point from which he can assail the trout that was noticed rising at the tail of the main stream. A few more steps then bring him to the far bank.

To fish a stream or length of river systematically, crossing and recrossing, each time a few yards higher up, until the whole has been thoroughly covered, takes time ; but it is far better that the angler's flies should be on the water, searching every spot fit to hold a fish, than waving in the air while he moves rapidly on from stream to stream. Particularly is this the case in Spring when the rise comes on late and ends early, and also on a Summer's evening when the water seems literally alive with fish, so madly do they rise, but for all too brief a spell. Time is of all importance on such occasions, and here it is that the angler who fishes methodically and with intelligence scores so heavily as compared with the rod who spends half his time in walking from stream to stream, and the other half in fishing them in a mechanical sort of way. So many unsuccessful fishermen only fish the larger streams of a river (and usually downstream), entirely ignoring the fact that, while such streams afford a harbour for a great number of fish, they are often deserted in favour of odd corners and favourite " lies " directly the " rise " begins.

The thoughtful fisherman studies the water, its

pools, currents and eddies, and all those other details, the meaning of which under varying conditions he has learned to read, and he is always alive to gather some new hint. He brings to his aid the wisdom gained by past experiences, successes and failures, and a knowledge of the habitat of the trout which has been the reward of keen observation and a reasoning mind.

He will tell you that in early Spring the trout, having hardly recovered their energy after spawning, are not to be found in the heavy rapids, but may be looked for at the tail ends of streams and in gently flowing water ; that, as the weeks go by, and as the sun's rays warm the water, insect life becomes more plentiful, and that the trout, once more lusty and strong with the abundant supply of food, spread themselves over the river, into rapid streams and all those places into which steady supplies are concentrated ; and further, that during the heat of Summer they will be located in the thinnest of water, at the very edges of streams, pools and eddies, where they lie ever ready to dart away at the least suspicion of danger.

Such an angler realizes the necessity of a good knowledge of insect life, watercraft and the habitat of the trout, and becomes as intimate with each as an artist is with his colours. And as blue and yellow combined will make a green, so surely will the man who thoroughly acquires such knowledge be a long way towards being numbered amongst the elect.

A goodly dish of trout hardly come by is a great satisfaction to a man who has to fit in his fishing days when he can, but perhaps the greatest pleasure to the true disciple of Walton is the capture, after many failures and disappointments and under difficult conditions, of some wily old trout whose education, by the constant bombardment of his stronghold, has been brought to a high degree of finish. What memories of his capture crowd the mind when some chance word stirs the chords ! Perhaps he came from out a moorland stream when the snell wind flung back the spray from every sounding fall, or may be he stubbornly gave up his virile life on some sun-steeped day when first the daffodils proclaimed that laggard Spring had come to a waking country side. Whatever the memory, it is wholly delightful.

The charm of fly fishing is never ending and a great part lies in the infinite field for experiment open to him who runs. Every day some new feature is revealed ; and, even in this twentieth century, he who will leave the beaten track, bent on exploration, will always discover new ground for investigation. The truth of this was brought home to one of the writers most forcibly when on a fishing expedition one July some years ago.

Rain on the previous day had left the river slightly coloured, and in magnificent condition, and as the sun was some little way above, though nearing the horizon, he, with the lightest heart and full of hope, approached a steady flowing reach where the banks were here and there fringed with clumps of willows.

A fish rose well out in the stream, then another, and another ; and as the tackle had been fitted up before leaving the farm-house, even to the putting on of a cast of flies, it was not long before those fish, which were apparently seizing every fly that passed over them, were covered again and again. All to no purpose, for the trout proved very discriminating, and at last, when a fish half rose without breaking the surface of the water, a change of fly was decided on.

Hovering round the willows, dancing to and fro in the air, were hundreds of insects, which on examination proved to be Light and Dark Silverhorns. Five minutes had barely elapsed when, with a Light Silverhorns to replace his point fly and a Dark one as first dropper, the angler was again assailing his fish ; but he could get no more satisfactory response than a bulge or two. Then the position of these two flies was reversed, a step which often pays, but it did not on that occasion.

The case was becoming desperate, for the rise would soon be over. So with some reluctance he left the rising fish and waded into the stream and put his flies into a likely looking eddy below an overhanging willow bush growing on the far bank. Almost immediately a fish was battling for dear life, but without avail ; and soon five more, all coming from under the bank, quickly joined him in the creel.

As the last of these fish was being drawn over the net, two local anglers appeared on the scene. Neither had killed a fish, so a few precious moments were taken up in wading out and giving each one or two of the killing fly.

When the rise was over the angler counted eight brace of nice sizable fish, all but two being killed on the Silverhorns, the exceptions having fallen to the Brown Owl, which was probably taken for the Light Silverhorns. All came from under the willows and banks on a reach no more than fifty yards in length, but strange to say, the local men finished up without a fish to show between them.

Later on, when considering the events of the evening between the sheets, it occurred to the successful one, that the killing fly of the evening was a killing fly only so long as it was fished close to the banks near the willows, and in those places over which hovered the natural fly. The locals had evidently fished the fly out in mid-stream ; hence their clean creels.

The following day was a Day of Rest, and as this idea was after all but surmise, nothing was said to the two local fishermen, but the results of the next evening's fishing were awaited with considerable interest.

Conditions on the Monday proved to be very similar to those prevailing on the Saturday, and the results of the day justified the surmise, that the fish under the willows were feeding on such insects as hovered above them, every now and then to touch the water, while those out in mid-stream had no Silverhorns available and so confined their attention to the spent spinners, smuts and other flies, which were brought to them by the current.

If the solution of the problem that presented itself on that first evening be correct, then the killing power of a fly is often dependent on its being fished with due regard to the haunts of the natural insect it is supposed to imitate. What a field is here for investigation, and yet the matter is one upon which no hard and fast rules can be made. Prevailing conditions must be studied carefully. A cross-wind might obviously entirely alter the local conditions, and one would not look in such circumstances for flies in their usual haunts. On windy days the observant angler would probably find that the menu of the fish on the side from which the wind was blowing would include many Diptera or other land-bred insects, while the fish on the lee shore, would most likely be feeding principally on such insects of aquatic origin as happened to be hatching out at the time.

The foregoing merely serves to illustrate a few of the many considerations involved in this absorbing sport ; and in following up these problems many side issues of equal importance will be opened up.

If the beginner is dogged by disappointment and failure (and who can feel the utter bitterness of disappointment more than a fisherman ?), let him be advised to take heart of grace and not to blame the lowness of the water, the brightness of the day, thunder or any of the elements, for his lack of sport, but to say to himself, " What have I left undone that should have been done ? Where have I failed ? " For trout, like human beings, take their daily bread ; and it is up to the angler to find out when and where and in what shape. If the beginner will therefore reason out the causes of failure instead of making excuses for it, he will be more likely then and on future occasions to remedy his mistakes and to know the satisfaction of killing fish on a really difficult day.

DRY-FLY FISHING.

Next to be considered are the dry fly and its use on the North Country Rivers ; but the novice is strongly urged, before ever he seeks to master this branch of angling, to get a good grip of the wet-fly method.

From the term "North Country Rivers" are naturally excluded such rivers as the Costa, which is probably the nearest approach in the North to the Chalk streams of Hampshire, the home of the dry fly. On that particular river the dry fly would probably on most occasions take the premier position, whereas on the rougher and more rapid streams, such as the Wharfe, Ribble, Lune, etc., the position is reversed.

Not many years ago one very seldom came across anyone further North than Derbyshire fishing the dry fly, but slowly and surely has the method become more and more popular ; for it is only by the judicious combination of the two methods of fly fishing that the best results and the greatest pleasure can, in the judgment of the writers, be obtained. But *chacun à son goût*, and far be it from them to legislate for any sportsmen who wish or agree to keep their waters exclusively for any one method of fishing.

Dry-fly fishing, as practised in the South, differs slightly from the method here advocated for the rougher streams above-mentioned, inasmuch as the purist of the South will not throw a fly to any but a rising fish, even though he wait an hour or more before locating one, while the North Country angler not only throws to the rise, but also to such places as are likely to hold feeding fish.

When a specially strong hatch of duns takes place on Northern rivers and the fish line up to suck in the insects as they hurry downstream, sails spread to the breeze, it will pay the angler to try the floater. Again, between streams on rapid rivers one often comes upon a long stretch of quiet steady flowing water ideal for the dry fly. By applying themselves to such a stretch with the methods of their friends of the South the writers have more than once retrieved a bad day. Quiet eddies too may frequently be fished with success by this method, and every river has some places, and is subject to some moods, in which the dry fly scores over the wet.

The first experience of one of the writers in dry-fly fishing was years ago. He had fished for grayling till noon on a bright frosty October day with indifferent success, when, on reaching a long stream with the current under the far bank, he noticed several fish rising at the tail. In between himself and the fish was a wide stretch of water some twelve or eighteen inches in depth, and the fish were out of reach, as the angler was not wearing waders.

Now the occasional fish he had managed to reach during the course of the morning absolutely refused the wet fly.

At the moment another fisherman appeared from upstream and, wading out, immediately caught several nice fish, to the no small envy of him on the bank. Before passing on the successful angler vouchsafed the remark " dry fly," and gave the writer in question the " oil tip " in theory and in practice.

Off came boots and stockings, and, with the shallow water safely waded, the rising grayling were within casting distance. So long as the fly—a Red Tag—could be kept dry, so long did the fish rise at it, but they would not look at it when water-logged. Between whiles

the angler came to shore to stamp a bit of feeling into his
legs, for the water was icy cold ; but he enjoyed himself
hugely and got quite a decent bag, besides adding greatly
to the scope of his accomplishment in the gentle art.

The writers have seen the dry fly score heavily
during the rise of Iron Blue Duns, and they remember
one occasion when that most dainty and beautiful
Ephemera was sailing down in numbers, and when a
feathered imitation accounted for six brace of fish
from a weed-grown reach of steady flowing water.

A word here must be said with regard to the timing
of the strike when using the dry fly, for the man who
is used to wet-fly fishing will probably strike too quickly
and at the most only prick his fish.   In the former
method, before attempting to drive home the steel,
the fish should be allowed to turn with the fly in his
mouth.   In wet-fly fishing the fish has often turned
before the rise becomes apparent.

Many occasions could be mentioned on which the
dry fly has given the writers most pretty fishing.
Once on a Cleveland stream, slow flowing and edged
with most luxuriant vegetation, the wet fly, cast over
rise after rise, was totally ignored, but a change to a
floating Female Black Gnat at once worked wonders.
Had it not been for the innumerable derelict branches
and water weeds in which the cast was time after time
tied up, the creel would have been heavy.   But the
enjoyment was intense that glorious June evening.

Quite sharp streams too will often fish well with the dry fly in the long evenings, and on one occasion it was again the Female Black Gnat which accounted for some difficult Wharfe trout that refused all wet flies, however presented. It is indeed during the evening rise that the dry fly will be found most generally useful on Northern streams.

That fickle evening rise that so many anglers impatiently wait for all day, only to return home beaten and disappointed at dark ! Not that the fish do not rise, for at times the water literally boils with them, but their discrimination is truly wonderful. How many an angler on occasions during all that mad rise has never killed a fish, or not until the sun had dropped well behind the horizon and dusk was upon him. Then perhaps he has creeled four or five before the rise ceased, but has returned home dissatisfied, realizing that he had been thoroughly beaten, and that it was the failing light, and not his skill, knowledge or ingenuity, that saved him from a blank.

An autopsy will often reveal on such occasions spinners, gnats and sedge flies ; and yet the most lightly and carefully made imitations, however deftly thrown, utterly fail as wet flies to attract the fish.

At times like these a Black Gnat, Ginger and Red Spinners No. 35 and No. 36, fished dry, and later, as the sun drops behind the horizon, a Silver Sedge may be recommended.

The angler should begin at the tail end of the stream and work gradually up, placing his fly over every rise and in all such places as are likely to hold feeding fish.

On occasions when all else fails, a trial may be given to a fancy fly, such as the Pink Wickham or Coachman. With such patterns during that most tantalising of rises the writers have sometimes retrieved their fortunes. Then, as dusk comes on and the dry fly becomes difficult to see, let the angler quickly change to a cast of wet flies, the flies dressed a size larger than those usually used during the day, and before the rise is over his creel may be the heavier for the change.

The dry fly has done yeoman service on some of those impossible days when fish streak away like lightning directly the cast falls on the water. By much stalking and careful fishing of out-of-the-way places and odd corners, the writers have sometimes finished with a brace or two which have given great satisfaction.

It is very comical to see the evident surprise of a fish which is taken in by a dry fly when he is quietly feeding in the shallows. Before he moves off for the stream he often seems to completely lose his head, bouncing about half in and half out of the water, and creating no end of a splash. On one occasion within the writers' experience under such circumstances a trout landed himself high and dry on the shingle where he broke the hold, and, continuing his antics, regained the water. Long ere this he must have made room for his descendants, as agile, let it be hoped, as himself.

How inordinately fond trout must be of the " fisherman's curse "—a term which covers, no doubt, several varieties of fly—for it will be found to have occurred in the trout's menu with unfailing regularity throughout the summer and autumn. It almost always is the fly which the trout pick off the surface of the water when they rise in the quiet flats the livelong day, days which, most anglers will agree, are usually the most difficult. Sometimes something may be done with Ginger or Red Spinners, wet or dry, under such conditions, when imitations of the " curses," probably on account of their size, fail to attract.

The Ginger and Red Spinners described have only by degrees worked their way into the inner circle of the writers' flies. Experience has proved their usefulness, for they will often be taken when all else fails. These dry patterns have killed fish under particularly difficult and hopeless conditions ; and their use is recommended with the greatest confidence.

Such then is a brief outline of the occasions on which the dry fly has been found to be of most use to the North Countryman ; but no hard and fast rules can be made, for the angler's discernment must play the greater part in regulating his actions, and the foregoing hints are merely given as some small guide to the beginner. But let all who try the dry fly beware of drag ; it will ruin the chances of the most artistic cast.

Anyone with designs on dry-fly fishing on Northern streams may well confine himself to a few of Mr. Halford's patterns, say the Olive Dun, Dark Olive Dun, Iron Blue Dun, and Black Gnat, with the addition of the Ginger and Red Spinners, Nos. 35 and 36, the Red Quill, and the Silver Sedge, and a fancy pattern or two, such as the Coachman and Pink Wickham, for use on occasions described above.

A great debt of gratitude is due to those who introduced the dry fly and developed its use so wholeheartedly, for there is a charm about dry-fly fishing which is distinctive, and a fascination that almost defies description in watching a neatly cocked artificial fly approach the rings made by a rising trout. A moment of suspense, intense excitement, followed by joy supreme when a timely strike is rewarded by a tightened line. So, apart from its being an asset in the filling of the creel, the dry fly increases the pleasures of the gentle craft to a very great extent, a craft as unique in its scope and variety as it is intriguing in its difficulties. The whole setting of the craft enhances its enchantment and give it a hold upon its followers, powerful as that of friendship, converting them into ardent devotees for life. Whether one follows its

Photo by   Mr. F. Brady

Broken Water

calling in the flower-starred water meadows of the South, or explores the rivers of the "stone-ribbed North," the peace and beauty of the surroundings, far from the noisy crowd, add a charm which every good fisherman knows how to be thankful for.

How pleasant is the time of the after-luncheon pipe, with the dipper curtseying from the stones in mid-stream. May be the desolate call of the curlew floats down from the fells, and the grey dale village, with its quaint architecture, speaks of times long past, of times when the Borderers filed down the valley, perhaps to fall upon a party of Monks from the rich Abbey of Fountains. Imagination suggests to the ear the savage shout of exultation of the assailants and the screams of the stricken, when a widening circle in the stream brings one back to present day realities in a second.

Such is a part of the angler's day, which, lingering in the mind, inspires him through the long wintry months to look forward to the time when God's earth shall be fresh and green again, and the wild thyme be fragrant on the banks of many a North Country stream.

Great men and small alike are held by the wonderful fascination of the sport, which gives such joy, affords such relaxation to the mind, and is so free from all taint of brutality. And though the actual angling requires the utmost concentration of mind and thought, yet after all, it has truly been described as " The Contemplative Man's Recreation."

CHAPTER III.

CREEPER AND STONE FLY FISHING.

THERE are not many streams in the North that have a distinct rise of May Fly or Green Drake, and for that reason the writers have not given any dressings of that fly, nor do they propose to devote space to a consideration of May Fly fishing. To make up for the loss of that beautiful Ephemera there is on most of these rivers the sober-hued Stone Fly, whose season almost coincides with that of the May Fly.

The flies are very different. The one, elegant and dainty, is to be seen one moment floating with wings upright upon the surface, then drifting in the breeze, while the other, dark coloured and of unprepossessing aspect, merges from the Creeper stage only to scuttle under the stones and remain quietly in darkness till nightfall, making off once more for obscurity if by chance its whereabouts is revealed.

The Stone Fly has four wings, which in repose are folded flat over the back. It passes the greater part of its existence in the Creeper state, in which it can be found during the latter part of April and throughout May under the stones in shallow water near the edges of streams. The Creeper varies in colour from an olive green to a dull dark brown, strong yellow showing at the junction of the segments of the body. It is of somewhat repulsive appearance, and measures from half an inch to nearly an inch in length. It has six legs, two caudal setæ, and two antennæ.

It is often difficult to collect a supply of Creepers ; not that they are particularly active, but the disturbance of the water caused by lifting the stones is apt to hide them while they wriggle under other stones. It is stated that if the angler, wishing to secure a supply, stands with his back to the current of the river and holds his landing net upright before him with the top of the net resting on the river bed, and then shuffles his brogues amongst the stones, the Creepers displaced by his activity will be washed into the waiting net and a plentiful supply be thus secured. The writers have never been particularly successful in this device, but that is no reason why others should not try it. The Creepers obtained are best kept in a tin box, together with a little damp moss.

There is no doubt that the Creeper forms an important item in the trout's menu in Spring, as an autopsy of the day's catch at that time of the year will reveal ; and many is the Creeper that has been grabbed by a watchful fish as it ventured from out its hiding place, or that has been torn from beneath the stones by a questing trout. Creepers are very plentiful in those North Country rivers which have the typical stony bed, but the season of the Creeper being April and May, the writers do not often fish it, nor is Creeper fishing generally much followed, as during that time of the year fly fishing is at its very best. Still, if on occasion the reader has found his most carefully dressed flies fail to rise a fish—as they will sometimes even in Spring—he might do worse than collect a few Creepers, as this method of fishing forms a pleasant variant of the fisherman's craft and throws a further light upon the habits and life and whereabouts of the trout.

The line should be well greased, and the cast (as in fly fishing), three yards tapered down to finest drawn gut with a form of Pennell tackle at the end, having the lower hook a size larger than the upper one (this latter being size No. 3 in the scale before mentioned on page 8). The bend of one hook should be five-eighths of an inch from the bend of the other, the hooks to be whipped on with olive green silk for preference. The fly rod and line complete the outfit.

The end hook of the tackle should be put through the Creeper almost at the extremity of its tail, where it is toughest, and the other hook in the unhappy beast's shoulder, not the head, as the head is liable to tear off.

The fishing should be done upstream and the Creeper cast gently, with an avoidance of jerk. The fly fisherman will soon instinctively feel the amount of power he can put into his casts. The rod point must be raised slowly as the bait trundles down, so that there is no drag. When the line stops or draws away, the angler tightens at once; otherwise the fish may eject the bait.

The most productive places in Creeper fishing are usually the edges of the streams, but rougher water and the necks of streams will often yield fish ; and all places where trout are known or expected to be should be tried, particularly about boulders and where a current in the river is contracted into a narrow run.

About the last week in May the Creepers will be found to be quitting the water and fastening themselves to the rocks and stones on the river's brim, to the buttresses of bridges, and to those rocks which stand out above the water. Here it is possible at times to watch the Stone Fly emerge through the slit in the back of the Creeper, leaving the perfectly-shaped skin rigid behind it, although in general Stone Flies hatch during the night.

Once the Fly is hatching in numbers, the carnival begins, although very few are to be seen unless they are searched for. An odd fly may be seen occasionally being carried down the stream or paddling across a shallow, but for the most part the Stone Flies lie very close in their hiding places beneath the stones near the water. Consequently the ideal conditions for Stone Fly fishing are when a fresh of a few inches comes suddenly down the river and washes them out of their hiding places.

The large females with the long wings are usually preferred by both fishermen and trout ; the fishermen find them easy to see on the water, and the trout no doubt find them a satisfying mouthful. The males vary in size, although they are smaller than the females and have shorter wings ; the smallest males are difficult to see when cast on the water and soon become water-logged ; the larger males are almost as good as the females. The males are called " Jacks." If males are used, the hooks of the tackle should be nearer together than the hooks in the tackle usually used in Stone Fly fishing.

It is not as a rule difficult to collect a supply of Stone Flies, but the males greatly outnumber the females. As they are picked up they can be placed in one of the Stone Fly boxes sold for the purpose, a transparent one for preference. The tackle and rod line and cast for Stone Fly fishing are exactly the same as those described for Creeper fishing, and the fly should be put on the hooks in the same manner as the Creeper.

The fishing should again be upstream and the Stone Fly be cast as in Creeper fishing ; but, whereas the Creeper is fished under the water, the Stone Fly is fished on the surface, as it loses much of its attractiveness when waterlogged. It will stand a fair amount of knocking about, but jerks should be avoided, as tending to throw the fly off the hooks.

The Stone Fly accounts for some large fish, and sometimes those old warriors that have passed the regular fly-taking stage, and have become wily and big, succumb to its charms. Therefore it is well to remember that all places which harbour a trout will often yield one under proper conditions ; and, although the streams fish about as well with Stone Fly as with anything else, it should not be forgotten that trout, when on the feed, very often leave the streams for shallow water, and for any vantage point where the current concentrates all the flotsam and jetsam from yards above into one narrow channel, and that they love to haunt the neighbourhood of rocks and boulders.

The Stone Fly will kill many fish which are not strictly on the feed, but which cannot resist the temptation to make the most of the Stone Fly season when a great juicy female fly floats overhead. If the reader bears this fact in mind he will seize the opportunity in the early summer to get the big one which has so often waved a vanishing tail at his flies.

The size of the fly is against its being sucked in as easily as the usual artificial, and it is of advantage to give a moment's grace before striking when a fish rises. Never to be forgotten is the disappointment of

a too hasty strike one lovely early June morning.
The angler was out before the sun topped the fell,
and a few brace were already in the creel, when he
reached a perfect eddy at the side of the main stream.
The Stone Fly was cast *secundum artem* (would that
the further proceedings had been on the same plane !).
It had hardly alighted when a big fish came up like a
porpoise. Alas ! quick as light the eager one tightened
without allowing the moment's grace, down went the
fish and played strongly, facing the current and giving
heartrending jars to the line. Confidence was beginning
to take the place of fear of a light hold, when up the
beauty came, headed into the stream and came down
with all the force of its waters thrown into the scale.
He was just opposite the angler when the rod flew up,
and that sorrowful angler saw no more of what would
undoubtedly have been his big fish of the season.

The charm of Stone Fly fishing is truly enhanced
by the season of its use. What could be finer than
the river side in the latter days of May and early June ;
and a turn before breakfast at that time of the year
is a delight to be remembered the winter through.
Besides, a good creel when fish are not so terribly difficult
to kill is like all success honestly come by, a delight
to the heart and a pleasure to one's friends.

CHAPTER IV.

UPSTREAM WORM FISHING.

NO book devoted to the subject of the fishing of North Country rivers would be complete without a chapter on worm fishing.

This branch of the sport, has during recent years become more and more popular in the Northern Counties, as worm fishing, under the conditions mentioned later, undoubtedly deserves to be classed as an art alongside of the highest forms of fly fishing. Indeed, in its difficulties it exceeds fly fishing, both wet and dry.

There remains, however, still a certain amount of prejudice against worm fishing among fly fishermen, who continue to look upon it as unsporting and therefore beneath the notice of a self-respecting fisherman. But the prejudice of these men is probably largely due to their misconception of the term. For while trout can mostly be caught by any in a fresh with very elementary tackle, it takes an observant and persevering man to make a basket under conditions suitable for sporting upstream worming.

The use of the worm during the first few months of the season cannot be defended, whether the river be low and clear, or running strong with the Spring freshets; for seldom a day passes at that time of the year without a rise at some part of it during which trout will take a fly, and, while that is the case, what true disciple of Walton would use any other lure?

The season therefore when the worm can fairly be used is restricted to the time of low clear waters during the hottest part of the summer, when the trout have ceased to rise freely to the fly in the day-time, a period of some eight or ten weeks, beginning about the 10th of June. The Stone Fly is usually over by that date. Any antipathy to worm fishing under those conditions in our North Country Rivers is difficult to understand, for it provides a most sporting variety of fishing during the blazing days of summer when the fly is hopeless. And unless a man is prepared to work hard in the blistering sun, unless he has a good knowledge of the habits of trout, and is able to show a fair amount of skill, both in approaching his fish and in throwing the worm, his basket will be a light one.

Many are the days during the latter part of June and the month of July when the man who fishes fly only will return home with but an odd fish or so to show for his day's outing. That may satisfy the gentleman of leisure, but to those who can devote to their favourite pastime only such days—often few and far between—as can be snatched from business, the killing of a few brace will appeal strongly.

To them in particular this chapter is addressed in the hope that some of those who, through prejudice, use fly only will reserve judgment, and, having read so far, may be sufficiently interested to read to the end of the chapter, and maybe to put into practice those hints which are here offered on one of the most delightful branches of trout fishing.

A day with the upstream worm always gives to the writers the utmost pleasure and satisfaction. Each cast is as full of interest as a cast made with the wet fly ; and from the moment the worm touches the water to the moment it is withdrawn, the excitement rivals that conjured up by the approach of a dry fly to the spot whence recently emanated the rings made by a rising trout.

Then again, the skill necessary to throw a worm without flicking it off the hooks, and to drop it exactly where required with the least possible disturbance, is of no mean order.

That is not all, however ; conditions vary, and all rivers from day to day present new problems. Unless therefore the angler is able to adapt himself to varying conditions, the most precise and delicate casting is of little avail.

To divine instinctively where the trout lie is the great secret of success; and it is the application of that knowledge that marks the expert in this branch of angling. To put the matter in a nutshell, an adept in upstream worm fishing combines delicate and accurate casting, unsurpassed even by the dry-fly man, with an intimate knowledge of the habits of trout. This can only be gained by keen and careful observation.

Neither wet-fly nor dry-fly fishing requires quite such a wide experience with regard to the habits of trout, and for that reason upstream worm fishing is to be classed as an art in itself. The knowledge gained of the habitat of the trout by clear water worming is a valuable asset to the wet-fly fisher and may often be turned to good account on one of those days when the hatch of fly is meagre and rising fish are few.

Is not this latter reason alone sufficient recommendation to induce every fly fisher to take up this branch of the art? If the reader thinks so, perhaps the few following hints on tackle and procedure may serve as some guide, particularly if he be a novice and about to make his initial effort.

The rod is, of course, of primary importance. Many writers recommend one of 12 ft. in length; and Stewart, who has always held the reputation of being one of the finest exponents of upstream worming of his day, recommends the use of a rod even longer than that.

No doubt a long rod has the advantage of enabling the wielder to keep out of sight readily, but the writers seldom use any other than a 10½ ft. fly rod, simply because they frequently find it advisable to change from worm to fly and *vice versâ*.

The reel and line should be the same as that used for fly fishing, and also the cast (as in fly fishing), a tapered one of three yards, the last yard being of finest drawn gut. Then comes the worm tackle. With regard to this there is a choice of three different varieties, each having its own advantages, and it is for the reader to use that with which he best succeeds.

First there is the single-hook tackle, in which the worm is threaded over the shank of the hook, and is kept from slipping down by a crank at the top. The advantages of this tackle are that most of the hook is hidden, being buried in the worm, and, the hook being fairly large, a good hold is got upon a fish when hooked.

Second comes the two-hook or Pennell tackle. In this case two small hooks are used, one being whipped on to the gut an inch above the other. The upper hook is put through the worm a quarter to half an inch below the head, the worm is then twisted once round the tackle between the hooks, and the lower hook is put through the lower end of the body. This is a very good form of tackle, and is the one preferred by the writers, as the worm lives longer on it than when threaded on a single hook, is livelier and has a more

natural appearance in the water.   The hooks should be
size No. 3 in the scale before mentioned on page 8.

Third comes the Stewart tackle, which is the same
in form as the Pennell, except that it has three hooks
one above the other, instead of two.   This is a tackle
the writers have very seldom used, and they are
therefore, perhaps, hardly competent to speak of its
merits.   Their experience, however, leads them to
think that the three hooks cannot be sufficiently well
concealed by the small worms which it is imperative to
use in low clear waters, and that therefore the trout
have a better opportunity of detecting the deception.

The next point in the outfit is waders, and these
are absolutely essential if the best is to be got out of
upstream worming.   The fish must be approached
from almost directly behind, which is impossible in
most cases if the fishing is done from the bank.

Lastly, the angler should always carry a few small
leads or sinkers which can be easily put on and easily
removed.   Split shot in various sizes, hammered flat,
will do quite well.   They will not often be required,
but it is always as well to have them handy for the
odd places where their use is necessary, which are
described later.

And now a word as to worms.   " Maiden dews," so
often advertised, are not the best for the purpose,
but those known as " Pinktails " are the real thing ;
they should be small, say 2 inches in length, and of

a pale pink colour. They should, of course, be well scoured, and they can be carried in moss in a bag hung round the neck.

With regard to throwing the worm, the two aims never to be lost sight of are accuracy and delicacy, and this combination can only be attained by constant practice. The man who can cast a fly will soon get the knack of putting the worm where he wishes, if he remembers that, when throwing the worm, the action is slower and more of a swing than in casting a fly, and that the rod point should be brought rather nearer the water at the finish of the cast. In addition to this, the arm should be pushed forward just as the worm is about a foot from the mark, in order to obviate any recoil and ensure that there shall be little disturbance of the surface as the worm drops into the water.

The greatest trouble of the novice is the frequency with which he flicks the worm off the hooks, particularly if the day's supply has not been well scoured. To master this trouble all jerks must be avoided, both when withdrawing the worm from the water and also when the cast is extended behind. As before stated, the movement should be more of a swing than in fly casting, with just sufficient power to extend the line behind and the same in front ; there will then be few lost or broken worms.

The next and, without doubt, the most essential point for consideration is where to fish.

Imagine a bright day towards the end of June on the banks of a typical North Country river. The gate just passed through brings one to the tail end of a rapid stream some fifty yards in length, broken here and there by boulders, some submerged and others just showing their dark mossy heads above the surface of the water. At the head of the stream there is a line of submerged stepping stones which no doubt many years ago, before the bed of the river changed, served a useful purpose.

This stretch of river from bank to bank is nowhere more than two feet deep, except in the middle a few yards below the stepping stones, where the current is strongest and where it has dug out a deeper channel. The beginner looking at this stream immediately notices the darker tone of water denoting the deeper channel and concludes that, of all places in the reach, that is the most likely to hold a good fish. Let him not be misled; the deeper channel holds many good fish, but of all parts of the stream, that channel is the least likely place from which to basket one.

Often have the writers seen men enter this stream, and wade straight out to the deeper water, unwittingly driving scores of trout in consternation before them. They fish the deeper rush of water, are rather surprised that it does not yield a fish, and then move up the river to the next stream, splashing right through the best water as they go. These men, more often than

Photo by N. N. Lee

The Head of the Dale

not, return home with a creel lighter than it was before they ate their mid-day meal ; and, besides doing nothing themselves, they make it absolutely impossible for another following on, to fish the stream with any chance of success within half-an-hour of their having disturbed it.

The way in which a friend, an adept at clear-water worming, would approach and fish this stream is very different.   Here is a description of his method.

He enters the reach at the very tail end, where, at the edge, the water ripples along some two or three inches deep.   The manner of his beginning may be compared to an otter's in the quietness with which he enters the river ; there is no splash or disturbance, and, more probably than not, he will stoop to avoid being seen.

He will make the first cast straight upstream, the worm entering the water twenty-five or thirty feet in front of him, but only some six to twelve inches from the bank.

Many beginners have laughed at the idea of a fish being caught in such a place, but let the unbelievers walk on a bright summer's day along the bank of a trout stream, and what do they see ?   Innumerable fish darting away from the edges of the river, scared at their approach.   It is for these very fish that our expert intends to try, when he makes his cast at the extreme edge of the river.

Directly the worm reaches the water, it begins to

travel naturally and without drag towards the angler,
who slowly raises the point of his rod, keeping in touch
with the worm so that a twist of the wrist will immediately drive the hook home if a fish takes hold. He
is careful to avoid drag, which is fatal, and is usually
caused by the too rapid raising of the rod point.
Without moving his position he makes another cast,
only this time slightly more across the stream, then
another and another, each being further from the bank.

He now wades gently a yard further upstream. In
front of him, and just within casting distance, he
notices an obstacle which causes a tiny eddy. The
object is little more than a good-sized tuft of grass
jutting out from the bank, but even that so alters
the flow of the water, as to form a likely feeding place
for a fish. The cast is carefully made and the worm
falls into the water as though it had crawled to the
edge of the grass and dropped in.

Almost as soon as the worm has touched the water
the current carries it gently, and quite naturally, into
the eddy. The line stops, our friend withholds his
hand, and it is not until the line moves slightly towards
the main stream that he gives a turn of the wrist,
driving the hook home into a nice half-pound fish.
For a moment it splashes dangerously in the shallow
water before making off for the deeper stream. The
hook, however, is well home and the captive is quickly
brought down and drawn over the submerged net.

" Well ! " says an uninitiated onlooker, " who would have thought that a fish would have been so near the edge, and in such shallow water too ? " The more you fish the upstream worm, the greater will be your astonishment at the number and the size of trout caught in such places.

Having basketed his fish, the angler rebaits his tackle, and then gently moves a yard further upstream, repeating his systematic casting. In this manner he stalks his quarry up the one side to the head of the stream. Yes, " stalk " is the word which most adequately describes this man's methods, as he takes the greatest pains to avoid being seen. It is work, and hard work too, on a blazing hot day ; but it pays, and it is only necessary to see the expert's basket at the end of it to be convinced. There is always a good dish of fish, and, as often as not, a very large fish to top off with.

The stepping stones having been reached, our friend leaves the water. Keeping well away from the edge he returns to the tail of the stream and wades some eight yards across. His first cast is made upstream and slightly towards the bank he has just left, the next one more directly in front, the next inclined towards the opposite side, and so on until he is casting more and more towards the far bank. Yard by yard the stream is covered in this manner, as the angler works upwards until two or three boulders are within casting distance, one showing distinctly above the surface of the water, while the others are detected only by the broken surface of the stream.

This is another very likely place, but our friend prefers the edges of the stream and thinner water to such places, although the latter are often good for two or three fish. The first cast is made towards the near bank, but without result. The second also fails to entice a fish, although the worm was dropped just by the side of one of the submerged boulders. At the third cast, however, which was made to the other side of the same boulder, a fish fastens and is brought to net. The golden gleam of another trout is seen as he is turned over, but missed, behind one of the other rocks. Then at the succeeding cast the worm enters the water about a foot beyond the rock which lifts above the surface of the stream. The sharp water running round the side of a boulder forms a favourite feeding place for a fish ; a trout occupying such a position usually lies with his head slightly in advance of the rock. The worm has just time to sink before it is picked up by the stream and carried rapidly down the run. A fish turns and darts after it. He seizes his prey as it sweeps almost past the rock, the steel is gently driven home, and another fish duly joins his brethren in the creel.

The whole of the stream is worked in the foregoing manner, the far edge of the river being treated in the same way as the side on which a beginning was made, and great care is taken that a tell-tale wave does not precede the angler.

At the far side, immediately below the stepping-stones, and lying slightly across stream, is the submerged trunk of an old tree which lodged there years ago, no doubt washed down and left by some winter flood. The position of this tree trunk, resisting the force of the current, causes a sharp stream to flow parallel to it. In this run a good fish will always be found, lying ready to seize whatever of his fancy the stream may carry to him. A cast is made, the worm gently dropping into the water some two or three inches from the side of the log. The rod point is slowly raised, our expert being most particular not to do this too quickly, and cause a drag on the worm. This necessity for avoidance of drag is a point to be reiterated and insisted on as strongly in this branch of the art as in fly fishing, as one is often inclined to think a stream is running quicker than is actually the case, and an unnatural drag will cause many a good fish to turn away, that would otherwise have taken the lure. The worm has hardly travelled more than half its course, when the line stops. As it moves away a gentle strike is rewarded by a tightened line, and another lusty trout is battling for dear life. Upstream he goes for a few yards, then flings himself into the air, but a lowered rod point defeats the manœuvre, and control of the captive is regained as he re-enters the water. The split cane soon tells on his strength, and quietly he is coaxed down stream to the net, but instead of floating in he merges indistinct into the shadowy water, and an upflying rod tells of a light hold and the loss of a stout-hearted fish.

Leaving this stream, and incidentally the friend whose methods have been studied, let the reader give his company up the river to the next stream ; and, to realize how failure may be caused by wrong approach, let him listen to an incident which happened to one of the writers in his early days of upstream worming. But first the stream must be described.

A long deep pool (or dub, as it is called on the Eden) breaks away in a short characterless rapid, narrowing towards the tail and then rushing under willow trees which hang right out over the river from the right bank. The strong stream has dug out a deep channel under these willows, while the left or near bank is a bed of fine gravel gradually sloping into the deeper water at the far side. This deep channel holds many good fish, but they are quite unassailable so long as they remain well under the willows.

Now for the incident. The day was blazing hot, the month July, and the river low and clear when the writer in question first essayed to fish it with the worm. Entering the water at the tail of the stream, he waded out as near as possible to the willows, which, as described, were on his left. Casting straight up in front of him he cherished the idea that the stream would carry the worm under the willows to the place where, it was hoped, the best fish would lie feeding. So far, so good. In this manner he worked to the top of the stream without a touch, when a final throw was made, pitching the worm into the water just where it rushed hardest under the willows.

Almost before the worm touched the water, the dark form of a large fish, some three or four pounds in weight, shot from the shallows on his right, to his holt in the deeps under the willows. This fish had been lying in the very thin water at the tail end of the rapids, no doubt seizing every morsel that came within reach, but ever ready to dart into his stronghold on the least sign of danger.

On the two following days the same thing happened, when it occurred to that youthful angler that his approach had been all wrong, and that if he had worked the thin water first, leaving the deeper channel until the last, success might have attended his efforts. But reflection had come too late ; he had to leave, and he never saw the fish again.

There is another moral to the incident ; although a deep inaccessible pool may be the stronghold of the largest trout, they will, during the hot summer months, frequently come to the thin edges of the stream to feed.

Another personal experience will perhaps serve to illustrate other possibilities. Towards the end of June, after seven weeks' drought, the writers went to the upper reaches of a North Country river, where, thanks to the generosity of the proprietor, they were permitted to have a few days' fishing. Owing to the long spell of dry weather the river, which at the best of times is there little better than a good sized beck, had shrunk to a mere trickle with deep pools here and there. The whole bed of the river was thickly coated with a green slimy growth.

Local opinion had it that fishing was waste of time until a good flood came to clean the bed of the river. Enthusiasm prevailed, however, as it was the first opportunity one of the party had of fishing this stretch, and the chance was not one to be missed, even though the prospects held out no great hope of success.

Up to about noon on the first day he who was strange to the water had never a fish to show for his efforts, although the trout were there and plentiful.

What with the oppressive heat and persistent failure, much of the keenness of early morning had worn off, and it was with a feeling akin to relief that the angler unslung his creel and threw himself on to the bank where he might enjoy a cigarette under the cool shade of the trees.

As the wreaths of smoke curled upwards, the unsuccessful one, with his back propped against the trunk of a tree, began to survey the stretch of river above him. Both banks were bordered by trees and clumps of willows for a distance of some two hundred yards. The water was nowhere more than two feet deep and so slight was the current that it was almost imperceptible. Not a ripple broke the surface of the stretch from end to end. It was like the proverbial " sheet of glass," and, had it but been able to reflect the expression on the angler's face, nothing but disappointment would have been revealed.

At length he jumped up with the intention of exploring the higher regions of the river and as he did so several fish, scared at his proximity, darted from the edge. Those trout decided the course of action, and, although the reach was to all appearances hopeless, the angler determined to try for some of the fish that were lying at the very edges, apparently basking in the sun.

Wading a stretch of water such as this, was most difficult, necessitating the utmost caution and slow approach, if the tell-tale wave were to be avoided. For obvious reasons it was essential that the angler should keep as close in to the willows on his side of the river as possible, and cast as long a line as he could control. Every time the worm was allowed to sink to the bottom, it was fouled with the vegetable growth on the stones. This happened almost every cast, and just as the angler was beginning to think that nobody but a fool would ever try to fish such a place, he came within casting distance of a narrow opening between the willows. Throwing carefully round the trees, the worm was landed within a few inches of the bank. There was a wave such as a trout makes when darting from the edge, and for the fraction of a second he thought that the slight disturbance caused by the worm dropping into the water had scared the fish. But no! the line quivered, then moved slightly, and, in response to a well-timed strike, the rod bent to the fight of a good half-pounder, which gave that thrill of satisfaction which is only felt when a difficult situation has been overcome.

That stretch of water yielded, within an hour or so, eight fish, which later proved to be above the average size for that part of the river.

The experience has been of the greatest value. Many times since then, when fish would not take well in the stream, has a blank been saved by attacking a stretch of water of this nature in this way. One thing leads to another, and perhaps a further use to which the knowledge gained on that occasion has been put is worth recording.

In common with many others, who can only go a-fishing at such times as business permits, the writers frequently wield the rod on most unpropitious days. Even in July they sometimes find on reaching the river that half a gale of wind is blowing dead down stream. An hour's battling against the elements, trying in vain to get the worm well up in front, is as a rule enough for anyone. Even if the worm lands occasionally where it is wanted, the wind will catch the line and cause a most unnatural drag, and ruin all chance of enticing a fish.

Those were the prevailing conditions on the first opportunity that offered of making use of the experience just narrated.

Leaving an ideal stream, which on this particular day was absolutely unsheltered from a strong downstream wind, the writers walked upstream, but had not gone far when one of them noticed, in contrast with the wind-beaten surface of the water, an unruffled place between two large trees which overhung the bank. The water here was wadable, the current almost nonexistent, and within the shelter of the trees it was not difficult to make a neat cast. The worm had scarcely touched the water when, from under the cover of the overhanging boughs, came a nice plump well-fed fish, and in full view of the angler appropriated the worm in the most unsuspicious manner. Enough, the angler walked on trying behind every bush, whether the river at that particular place was streamy or otherwise ; and since then, the writers have often had the laugh of a heavy downstream wind.

Now by the foregoing it is not desired to suggest, that it is wise, whenever an almost streamless stretch

of water is reached, to fish it, as the process is slow
and takes up much time, which might probably be
used to better advantage in the streams and thin
water ; but, as a stand-by, when conditions are against
the angler and the trout not keen, it is always well to
try such places.

Another favourite feeding ground, where innumerable trout always congregate, is the very tail end of a
pool, just before it breaks away into the stream below.
The water in such a place forms a glassy glide, in
fishing which the novice will find his path to success
beset with difficulties, particularly if the banks of the
river afford no cover. The greatest circumspection
in approach, and more than ordinary delicacy in
casting, are two essentials which will go far towards
the mastery of this situation ; but there is again
the difficulty of an unnatural drag to be overcome.
To obviate this trouble entirely in such a place, is
almost impossible, but much may be done to attain
the desired end by fishing with a short line and
letting as little of it touch the water as possible.
Reaches of this character, however, will always fish
best when the angler has the wind behind him, and
under those conditions should never be neglected, as
among the trout which haunt such places will
frequently be found the largest that the river produces.

Let it be understood, however, that the remarks
in the foregoing paragraph apply principally to large

pools extending almost the whole way across a river ; but at the same time, it must not be thought that the tail end of a small pool is useless ; on the contrary, such places will often yield a trout, and they are easier to fish than the larger glides.

Mention of the uses for the sinkers suggested in the outfit has been purposely left until almost the last, as in clear-water worming the part they play is a very small one.

When on an open stretch of water trouble is experienced in casting against a wind, after having first tried in vain to overcome the difficulty by reducing the length of the casting line, then, as a last resource, pinch on to the cast a small lead eighteen inches above the hooks. This will materially assist in getting out the line, and at the same time the lead will help to reduce the drag on the line which the wind will be certain to cause.

Further use for sinkers will be found when fishing rapid rivers where many channels of very swift flowing water are frequently met with. Outside these occasions, however, leads will be found of little value and their use should be exceptional in upstream worming.

Without wishing to enlarge further on this almost inexhaustible subject, there is one other point of some importance which should be mentioned and that is a method by which any difficulty experienced in detecting when the worm has been seized may be overcome. Many beginners, particularly if their eyesight is not of the best, find this a great source of trouble. Let them grease the reel line well before a start is made. It will then float, and any check upon it will be noticed immediately. If even that does not get over the difficulty, let them tie on a small piece of light-coloured wool where the cast and line join (the wool can often be obtained from the fences at the stream side where sheep have rubbed), form the wool into a tiny ball and soak it with oil such as is carried by the dry-fly man. When this ball gets water-logged all that is necessary is to squeeze it between finger and thumb and occasionally re-oil it. It will be found to float splendidly, and by following the golfer's first maxim, " Keep your eye on the ball," few bites will pass unobserved.

Let it be hoped that those who have read to the end of this chapter and feel any inclination to give clear-water worming a trial will get from that branch of the sport as much pleasure and satisfaction as the writers have enjoyed, during those days in summer which come, alas, all too seldom. Days which open with the incomparable freshness of a June morning, continue with the brightest of skies, with songs of birds, and murmuring streams, and close with the landscape wrapped in shadows. The while great beetles drone by, and moths, white and brown, flutter out of the grasses under foot, when it requires an effort to leave such a wonderful world, and to re-enter the dwellings of man.

CHAPTER V.

MINNOW FISHING.

MINNOW fishing, although barred on many streams, has much to be said for it, if it be practised judiciously and at certain times of the year, as it accounts for many of the larger fish whose cannibal habits have grown in proportion to their years, and whose demise can in no way be regretted. It may, therefore, fairly be said that the majority of Northern rivers are benefited by a limited use of the minnow. But its use must be *limited*, for it does a stream a great deal of harm, if, from one end of the season to the other, it is daily raked with minnows, natural and artificial, of all shapes and sizes. Besides, the practice is unfair to those who wish to fish the fly, as trout are usually put down for some considerable time after a minnow has been spun over them.

It is, moreover, a mystery why any man should wish to fish the minnow during the early part of the year when trout rise readily to the fly. Spinning should therefore be restricted to times of flood, as hereafter described, and to the latter part of the season, excepting September.

When fish begin to come somewhat shyly at the worm during July and August—fished in the method previously described—they are frequently in the right mood for a minnow. At such times the waters are usually low and clear ; it therefore requires considerable dexterity to achieve success, and there is no doubt that the minnow, fished under such conditions, is a sporting method of angling ; although it is a greater pleasure to land a pound trout on a 00 hook than to kill a two pounder on the heavier tackle required for minnow fishing.

With the evolution of the casting reel—its yearly improvements and new inventions, all in aid of long distance casting—there is reason to think that minnow fishing has been popularized at the expense of the skill shown by the old-fashioned school, which, using a short line and possessed of a good knowledge of the habits of its quarry, lured many an old cannibal from under the tree roots, from behind some boulder, or from the depths of an eddy, old villains that had battened for years upon the young stock of the river.

One sees now, not without regrets, little of the old manner of fishing the minnow, but far more of the method in which the minnow is thrown as far as possible across stream, and then worked back to the angler with very little idea of its being properly presented. The modern method appears to require but little skill, knowledge or ingenuity, and it is by a long way the nearest approach to " chuck and chance it " of any of the methods of fishing described.

The long-distance casting reel has its uses, but in minnow fishing, as in all other branches of angling, the man must adapt himself to circumstances, and if he does so he will find that it is not always necessary to throw a long way.

Out of all the reels on the market it would be presumptuous to say that such and such a reel is best. Each has its advocates, and while one man will swear by a certain make, the next may swear at it.

The rod should be short, 8 ft. 6 ins. or 9 feet, and fairly stiff, though not too stiff. If a preference may be expressed, it is for a rod that just gives slightly as a minnow is drawn across the current, and for light spinning the split-cane fly rod frequently serves very well.

The line to use with the majority of reels is made of fine waterproof silk, as it does not kink so readily as an undressed one, but there are certain reels on the market with which it is an absolute necessity to use undressed lines, and for many it is claimed that their mechanism can be so adjusted as to do away entirely with kinking.

Out of the many varieties of mount for the natural

minnow there is none so popular in the North (and deservedly so) as the " Ariel." It is easily baited ; the lead (which can be had in various weights) is pushed into the body of the bait, the bottom hook is put through the back just above the tail, and the gut is then drawn tight until a slight bend is imparted to the minnow ; the other hooks are then put into either side so as to hold the bait in position. There is one point of importance which must be carefully watched in baiting the tackle. The fore part of the minnow must be perfectly straight ; if this is not so and there is a curve in that part of the body, instead of spinning cleanly, the minnow will come towards the angler with an intoxicated wobble, which is fatal to good results.

The variety of artificial minnows offered to fishermen is truly bewildering, and life is far too short for the writers to have tested even a tithe of them ; but there is one which has invariably proved a killer in a coloured water, and that is the " Devon." It is sold in all sizes from one inch upwards and in a variety of colours. The virtues of this minnow lie, in all probability, in its particularly brilliant spin, and it is the writers' practice always to have two or three sizes handy, in gold, brown and blue.

To them it is a proven fact that the artificial is never so good as the natural ; for a trout if he once runs at an artificial, but is not hooked, will seldom

come again. Whereas with a natural minnow, once
the trout has tasted blood, he often cannot resist the
temptation to have a second go, unless he has been
badly scratched ; and in some instances, he will come
again and again until finally hooked. There are,
however, times when natural minnows seem more
difficult to get than trout ; and for a clear water on
such occasions, a light Phantom, or one of the many
excellent reproductions of the minnow sold by fishing
tackle houses can be used.

The trace should be from three to five feet in length,
the former being long enough for a coloured water,
and the latter short enough for the clearest conditions.
It should, for average use, be of finest undrawn gut,
though when using very small minnows in a low clear
water, a much finer quality is to be recommended.

To obviate kinking of the cast and line, and to get
a nice free spin, it is, of course, necessary to use swivels
on the trace. Of these the angler should always
carry a supply of various sizes, and at least two should
be put on to the cast. The writers' practice is more
often than not to use three, increasing slightly in size
as the distance from the minnow increases. And
in preference to the use of lead on the trace, they are
always for having it concealed in the body of the
minnow whenever possible.

The most silvery natural minnows are undoubtedly
the best. They should be from an inch and a quarter

to two inches in length, and they are perhaps better used fresh than in any other condition. If they are put into a bottle three parts full of water, corked, and carried in the pocket, they may be kept alive the whole day, if the water be changed occasionally.

If the angler is anxious to keep the weight of his impedimenta down to a minimum, salted minnows take up far less room than live ones and are naturally much lighter, and it is doubtful whether they are appreciably inferior to fresh ones. But preserved minnows, which have been kept in a solution of formalin, are certainly not so good as fresh or salted ones, as trout never seem to want to try a second bite, when they have been missed the first time.

Minnow fishing as practised in a coloured water is comparatively easy, and does not call for any great amount of dexterity. That branch of the sport, therefore, may be dealt with first, with the prefatory remark that the minnow at such times should be used judiciously and sparingly and with a view to removing the cannibals from the river.

When a fresh is running, the minnow is used to best advantage when the river begins to rise and again as it subsides, that is when it wears the complexion known as " porter colour." If on such occasions the angler sees an odd fish or two rise in some eddy or back wash, he may count the risers his if he spins with any skill at all.

If the angler knows of the stronghold of some

A Brook in Spring

Photo by   N. N. Lee

monster trout grown ugly and big on a diet of trout,
minnows and bottom food, let him hasten thither
with all speed if a fresh comes down the river, and
fish very carefully round the ancient's precincts, as
in all probability he will come from out his keep to
seek for food round the edges of the stream, and to
seize any fry which he sees carried down by, and
struggling against, the rush of the water.

To fish a coloured water, the angler must throw
his minnow well across stream and then bring it round
to his own side in a series of short pulls, occasionally,
where the current is strongest, allowing the force of
water to carry it a foot or two down stream, imitating
more or less what one would imagine the actions
of some small fish would be that had got into heavy
water. And as trout will often follow a minnow from
one side of the river to the other before taking it, and
as in flood time they are to be found under the banks
very close to the edge, it is imperative that the angler
should not lift the minnow out of the water until he
has worked it well up under the bank on which he
stands, and thoroughly searched the edges. It is
impossible to lay too much stress on this point,
as it will be found that almost eight fish out of ten
take the minnow close to the edge, just as they become
afraid that they may lose their prey.

All slack waters, eddies and places out of the rush
of heavy water, where trout seek shelter in time of

flood, should be fished ; and, if it be possible to cast
the minnow upstream and to work it down, the reward
will be greater than that gained by the man who will
not take the trouble to fish as recommended

The next point to consider is the strike, and it is
in minnow fishing that the angler's self-control will be
most highly taxed.   As soon as he feels a trout touch
the minnow, he will be tempted to strike—the novice
will probably give a startled jerk and ruin his chances
—but not until a trout has got a good hold on the
minnow should any strike be given ; and then it should
be more of a firm steady strain than what is generally
known as a " strike."

Minnow fishing in a clear water is very much more
artistic, and at the same time more difficult, than the
methods previously described, for it calls for precise and
delicate casting, and requires an intimate knowledge
of the habits of trout.   In the blazing days of late
summer it is very exhilarating to fish the minnow up
some small clear tributary stream or brook, at the
most only a few yards wide ; and to do so successfully
requires consummate skill.

In fishing waters of this description it is imperative
that the minnow be thrown directly upstream and
then rapidly spun down.   This latter point must be
attended to, otherwise the minnow coming down
more or less with the current, will not spin.   The
main stream, places under banks, about submerged

tree roots, and behind boulders, and the heads of rapid streams, should all be carefully searched, and when the angler observes a trout rush from its place of concealment at his minnow, he must keep a firm hold upon his nerves and simply continue steadily to spin without himself otherwise moving.

A trout bent upon the capture of a minnow becomes very unwary and will frequently follow his prey almost to the feet of the angler, and, if the angler remains as still as his spinning will allow, will often seize the bait at the last moment. It is very necessary therefore to fish a cast right out.

It is also wise in the main to adapt the size of the minnow, be it natural or artificial, to the size of the water to be fished ; and it should always be remembered that a minnow is better too small than too large. When fishing small tributary waters, or even thin water on the main river, the weight of the lead or sinker may be materially reduced, and a small minnow should be used.

When fishing the main river under low clear water conditions, *upstream* methods must be rigidly adhered to, and the beginner may here be warned, above all things, not to get into that mechanical method of fishing the minnow now so prevalent, which is satisfied with long casts across the river and recovery of line without any definite object in view, except to get the minnow from *one side to the other*.

If a boulder resists the onward flow of the current near the far bank, throw the minnow so that it drops gently into the water a foot or more above the boulder; then spin down past it. If nothing happens then, try the other side of the rock. Should the water undermine the far bank, drop the minnow in at the top of the run and spin down it; in fact try every place, including the thinnest of water, that could contain a fish, and use all the knowledge and intelligence you have; for you will need it all, if you are to get any success in low clear water.

When a reach of quiet steady-flowing water is ruffled by a wind, it will often yield good results to a minnow carefully fished. The edges should be thoroughly worked and the angler should never fail to spin his minnow alongside all patches of weed, as in such places minnows frequently congregate, and a feeding trout knows where to find them.

Another type of spinning is afforded by a long reach of rapid water that is broken up all over by boulders of every possible shape and size. In such water the trout will not follow the minnow far; they will either seize their prey as it passes them, or turn round and make a sudden rush at it before it can get many inches below. Therefore it is best to fish the minnow here with a short line and to spin the bait briskly down past each boulder. For such water the longer fly rod will be found to be the better weapon. The minnow is also sometimes useful when a gale of wind in the middle of summer puts fly fishing out of the question.

To be able to command success with the minnow, either in clear water or in brooks, is an accomplishment worth striving for. It is a sport that gives the fisherman excitement in plenty, as the whole actions of the trout are seen from beginning to end. And it is impossible to describe adequately the fascination which holds the angler whose eyes are riveted upon a fish rushing down upon his minnow, nor to tell the difficulty of refraining from incontinently snatching away the minnow from a fish in the act of seizing it.

Although minnow fishing has many attractions, when followed in times of bright skies and low waters, it is perhaps more open to abuse than any other of the fair methods of angling. For not only does the indiscriminate use of the minnow, especially with the long-distance casting reel in the hands of a persevering man—not necessarily a very skilful one—work havoc amongst the fish, but it spoils the sport of others, as a spun minnow usually puts fish down for some considerable time. Therefore, in Club waters particularly, a man should be careful and circumspect in the use of the minnow. For while its judicious use will do good in removing fish that can well be done without, and will sometimes provide a dish of trout when the fly is at a discount during the heat of the day, say, in August, its use out of season will call down many hard words. And while it is possible for one to work rapidly downstream, raking the whole river across and across and thus spoil the sport of all others on the water, a sportsman will choose his reach, fish it quietly upstream, and leave his brethren of the fly in peace and undisturbed enjoyment.

INDEX.

Across stream fly fishing, 39
Ant, Dressing for, 29
Ant, Season for, 14
Ariel Tackle, 94
Artificial Flies, See Flies
August Dun, Dressing for, 28
August Dun, Season for, 14
Autopsy, 34, 57, 63

Bites, Method of detecting in upstream Worm Fishing, 90
Black Gnat, 56, 57, 60
Black Gnat, Dressing for, 24
Black Gnat, Season for, 13
Bodies of Flies, 8, 10
Broughton's Point, Dressing for, 18
Broughton's Point, Season for, 13
Brown Owl, Dressing for, 20
Brown Owl, Season for, 13

Cast, 37, 64, 66, 73, 95
Cast, Gut, How to Taper, 38
Casts, Rapidity of in Wet-fly Fishing, 46
Casting Reel, 92, 93
Chalk Streams, 37, 42, 53
Chuck and Chance it, 42, 93
Coachman, 58, 60
Coloured Water, Size of Flies for, 10
Costa, 53
Creeper, Description of, 63
Creeper Fishing, Rod for, 64
Creeper Fishing, Tackle for, 64
Creeper, Method of Baiting, 64
Creeper, Method of Collecting, 63
Creeper, Method of Fishing, 65

Dark Needle, Dressing for, 19
Dark Needle, Season for, 13
Dark Olive Dun, 60
Dark Sedge, Dressing for, 25
Dark Sedge, Season for, 14
Dark Silverhorns, Dressing for, 28
Dark Silverhorns, Season for, 14
Dark Snipe, Dressing for, 17
Dark Snipe, Season for, 13
Dark Watchet, Dressings for, 20, 21
Dark Watchet, Season for, 13
Devon Minnows, 94
Diptera, 52
Dotterel, Dressing for, 22
Dotterel, Season for, 13
Downstream, When to Fish Fly, 40
Drag, 46, 60, 78, 81, 87, 88, 89
Dressings of Flies, 16 et seq.
Droppers, Dressed to Hair, 9
Dry Flies, List of, 60
Dry-Fly Fishing, Rod for, 37
Dry-Fly, Times for Fishing, 54
Dubbing, Mixture of, 9

Eden, 82
Entomology, 34
Evening Rise, 57
Evening, Size of Flies for, 58

Far-off and Fine, 45
Fisherman's Curse, 59
Flies, Bodies of, 8, 10
Flies, Dressed lightly, 10
Flies, Dressed to gut, 8
Flies, Dressed to hair, 8

Flies, Dressings of, 16 et seq.
Flies, Heads of, 10
Flies, Number on cast in Wet-fly Fishing, 36
Flies, Seasons of, 10, 13 et seq.
Flies, Size of, for Coloured Water, 10
Flies, Size of, for Evening Fishing, 58
Flies, Tables of, 13 et seq.
Flies, To err on small side, 10
Flies, Winged, 9, 11
Fly Dressing, McClelland's Book on, 7
Fly, Taking, Fished as point, 12
Formalin, Minnows preserved in, not recommended, 96

General Use, Rod for, 37
Ginger Spinner, Dry, Dressing for, 30
Ginger Spinner, Dry, Season for, 14
Ginger Spinner, Wet, Dressing for, 24
Ginger Spinner, Wet, Season for, 13
Gnats, 57
" Gossamer," Pearsall's Silk, 9
Gravel Bed, Dressing for, 23
Gravel Bed, Season for, 13
Greased Line, 64, 90
Green Insect, Dressing for, 29
Green Insect, Season for, 14
Greenheart Rod 36
Greenwell's Glory, Dressing for, 16
Greenwell's Glory, Season for, 13
Gut, Tapered Cast, 38
Gut, Flies dressed to, 8

Hackle Points, 11
Hair, Flies dressed to, 8
Halford, Mr. F. M., Patterns of Flies of, 60
Hardy's Hooks, 8
Heads of Flies, 10
Hickory Rod, 36
Hooks, 8, 64, 66, 73, 74
Hooks, Hardy's, 8
Hooks, Short in Shank, 8

Inner Side of Feather, 9
Insect Life, Knowledge of, 33, 34
Iron Blue Dun, 56, 60

" Jacks," 66
July Dun, Dressing for, 26
July Dun, Season for, 14

Kinking, 93, 95
Knotted Midge, Dressing for, 23
Knotted Midge, Season for, 13

Leads, 74, 89, 94, 95, 99
Light Needle, Dressing for, 21
Light Needle, Season for, 13
Light Sedge, Dressings for, 25
Light Sedge, Season for, 14
Light Silverhorns, Dressing for, 27
Light Silverhorns, Season for, 14
Light Snipe, Dressing for, 19
Light Snipe, Season for, 13
Lightly Dressed Flies, 10
Line, 37, 64, 66, 73, 90, 93, 95
Line, Short for Upstream Fly Fishing, 45
Line, To be greased, 64, 90
Lune, 54

Maiden Dew Worms, 74
March Brown, Dressings for, 18, 19
March Brown, Season for, 13
McClelland's Book on Fly Dressing, 7
Metamorphosis of Creeper, 65
Minnow Fishing, in a clear water, 98
Minnow Fishing, in a coloured water, 96
Minnow Fishing, in a wind, 101
Minnow Fishing, Rod for, 93, 100
Minnow Fishing, Season for, 92
Minnow Fishing, Tackle for, 94
Minnow Fishing, Upstream, 98, 99, 102
Minnow, Where to Fish, 96
Minnows, Better too small than too large, 99
Minnows, in Formalin, 96
Minnows, Method of Baiting with, 94
Minnows, Method of keeping alive, 96
Minnows, Natural better than Artificial, 94
Minnows, Salted, 96

Oil Tip, 36, 55, 90
Olive Bloa, Dressing for, 20
Olive Bloa, Season for, 13
Olive Dun, 60
Orange Partridge, Dressing for, 17
Orange Partridge, Season for, 13
Outer Side of Feather, 9

Pale Watery Dun, Dressing for, 27
Pale Watery Dun, Season for, 14
Pearsall's " Gossamer " Silk, 9
Pennell Tackle for Creeper and
    Stone-Fly Fishing, 64
Pennell Tackle for Upstream Worm
    Fishing, 73
Phantom Minnow, 95
Pinktail Worms, 74
Pink Wickham, 58, 60
Point Fly, 12
Poult Boa, Dressing for, 22
Poult Bloa, Season for, 13
Primary Feathers, 9

Rapidity of Casts in Wet-Fly
    Fishing, 46
Red Quill, 60
Red Spinner, dry, Dressing for, 30
Red Spinner, dry, Season for, 14
Red Spinner, wet, Dressing for, 26
Red Spinner, wet, Season for, 14
Reel, 37, 73, 92, 93
Ribble, 54
Rod for Creeper Fishing, 64
Rod for Dry-Fly Fishing, 37
Rod for General Use, 37
Rod for Minnow Fishing, 93, 100
Rod for Stone Fly Fishing, 66
Rod for Upstream Worm Fishing,
    73
Rod for Wet-Fly Fishing, 36
Rough-Bodied Poult, Dressing for,
    27
Rough-Bodied Poult, Season for, 14

Salted Minnows, 96
Season of Flies, 10, 13 et seq.
Secondary Feathers, 9
Sedge Flies, 57
Short-Bodied Flies, 8
Short Line for Upstream Fly
    Fishing, 44

Silk, Pearsall's " Gossamer " 9
Silk, Shades of, 9
Silk, Waxed, 9
Silver Sedge, 57, 60
Single Hook Worm Tackle, 73
Small Side, Artificials to err on, 10
Smuts, 52
Spinners, 8, 52, 57
Spinners, Wing for, 11
Spinning, Rod for, 93, 100
Split-Cane Rod, 37, 93
Split Shot, 74, 89
Spring Black, Dressing for, 17
Spring Black, Season for, 13
Stewart, Rod recommended by, 72
Stewart Tackle, 74
Stone Flies, Females, 66
Stone Flies, Males, 66
Stone Fly, Description of, 62
Stone-Fly Fishing, Rod for, 66
Stone-Fly Fishing, Tackle for, 66
Stone Fly, Method of Baiting, 66
Stone Fly, Method of Fishing, 66
Stone Midge, Dressing for, 23
Stone Midge, Season for, 13
Strike, Timing of, 41, 56, 65, 67,
    78, 81, 86, 98
Swivels, 95

Tackle for Creeper Fishing, 64
Tackle for Minnow Fishing, 94
Tackle for Stone-Fly Fishing, 66
Tackle for Upstream Worm Fishing,
    73, 74
Tail of Pool, Upstream Worm
    Fishing of, 88
Taking Fly, Fished as Point, 12
Tapered Cast, How to Make, 38
Trace, 95
Transparent Wax, 9

Under Side of Wing of Artificial, 9
Upstream Fly Fishing, 41
Upstream Fly Fishing, Short Line
    for, 44
Upstream Minnow Fishing, 98, 99,
    102
Upstream Worm Fishing in still
    water, 85
Upstream Worm Fishing, Method
    of, 76

Upstream Worm Fishing, Method of detecting Bites, 90
Upstream Worm Fishing, Rod for, 73
Upstream Worm Fishing, Season of, 70
Upstream Worm Fishing, Secret of Success in, 72
Upstream Worm Fishing, Tackles for, 73, 74
Upstream Worm Fishing, Wrong Method of, 82

Vibrate Rod Point, 41

Waders for Upstream Worming, 74
Waterhen Bloa, Dressing for, 16
Waterhen Bloa, Season for, 13
Wax, Transparent, 9
Waxed Silk, 9
Wet Flies, Number on Cast, 36
Wet-Fly Fishing, Methods of, 39

Wet-Fly Fishing, Rod for, 36
Wharfe, 54, 57
Wind, Effect of, on Haunts of Flies, 52
Wind, Upstream Worm Fishing in a, 87
Wing for Spinners, 11
Wing of Artificial, under side, 9
Winged Flies, 9, 11
Winter Brown, Dressing for, 16
Winter Brown, Season for, 13
Wool on Cast in Upstream Worm Fishing, 90
Worm Tackles, 73, 74
Worms, 74

Yellow-Legged Bloa, Dressing for, 22
Yellow-Legged Bloa, Season for, 13
Yellow Partridge, Dressing for, 21
Yellow Partridge, Season for, 13

Printed by Percy Lund, Humphries & Co., Ltd., Priestman Street, Bradford, and 3, Amen Corner, London, E.C.   24422